LORD,

I NEED GRACE TO
MAKE IT TODAY

LORD,
I NEED GRACE TO MAKE IT TODAY

A DEVOTIONAL STUDY *on* GOD'S POWER

for DAILY LIVING

KAY

ARTHUR

WATERBROOK
PRESS

LORD, I NEED GRACE TO MAKE IT TODAY
PUBLISHED BY WATERBROOK PRESS
12265 Oracle Boulevard, Suite 200
Colorado Springs, Colorado 80921
A division of Random House, Inc.

Unless otherwise indicated Scripture quotations are taken from the *New American Standard Bible®*. (NASB).© Copyright The Lockman Foundation 1960, 1962, 1963, 1968, 1971, 1972, 1973, 1975, 1977. Used by permission. Scripture quotations marked (KJV) are taken from the *King James Version* of the Bible.

ISBN 1-57856-441-7
     (previously 0-88070-881-6)

Library of Congress Cataloging-in-Publication Data

Arthur, Kay, 1933-
    Lord, I need grace to make it today : a devotional study on God's power for daily living
    / Kay Arthur.— 1st WaterBrook Press ed.
        p. cm.
    Rev. ed. of: Lord, I need grace to make it.
    Includes bibliographical references (p.).
    ISBN 1-57856-441-7
        1. Grace (Theology) I. Arthur, Kay, 1933- Lord, I need grace to make it. II. Title.

BT761.3 .A78 2001
234—dc21   00-068624

Printed in the United States of America
2005

10 9 8 7 6 5 4

This book is dedicated to two very special people in my life.

*To my husband, Jack, who knows what it is to live in the grace of God
day in and day out, because he lives with me!
How I thank this godly man for letting me fulfill the ministry
to which our Lord has called me.*

*To Evelyn Wheeler, my daughter in the Lord. This book first became a
reality through her vision and selfless dedication.
How I thank God for her…
the daughter I wanted but never physically gave birth to!*

CONTENTS

For the grace of God has appeared,

bringing salvation to all men.

TITUS 2:11

INTRODUCTION

At times we all wonder if we are going to make it—or if it is even worth the trying, the effort, the fight. The pressure, mental or physical, seems relentless. It's the "same ol', same ol'," and it is wearing. Very wearing. Why not just lay down and give up?

Lay down and give up? We can't—because His grace is there, offered freely, given *today* freely and lavishly for all who would take it.

Yet the problem is that we don't always know how to seek and find that grace—or after knowing how, we forget and need to be reminded. That, Beloved, is what this devotional study is all about. It's about crying out to God, "Lord, I need grace to make it today," and then finding out how to appropriate His grace for any and every situation you will face and every feeling you will have to deal with.

That is why this book is set up this way. For the next nine weeks, you are going to immerse yourself day by day in the warm, stress-relieving water of God's Word. The aches, the pains, the tension, the stress will gradually subside as you find yourself resting in the sufficiency of His grace. On some of the days there will simply be a truth to examine and embrace; other days there will be things you want to look up, study, and write out. But always there will be application to where you are today.

This is a devotional study that will minister to you in intimate, personal ways—but it is also a book that, when shared and discussed with a group, will take on even new depth as you learn from one another—and as you help one another learn to appropriate His grace day by day.

If there's a possibility of your using this as a group study in which you would be a facilitator, then read "Guidelines for Group Use" in the "Study Resources" section at the back of this book, where you'll find other valuable tools to enhance this study.

For many, the blessing of this study has been enhanced by the companion video and audio teaching tapes. For more information on these, simply call Precept Ministries International at our toll-free number (1-800-763-8280) and let one of our staff members help you. It would be their pleasure. We also provide training if you would like to develop your skills in handling the Word of God more accurately or in leading others in group studies designed to minister to people of all ages at any level of commitment while respecting the restraints on their time. We're known as "The Inductive Study People: everybody, everywhere, any time, any place, any language, any age. One message: the Bible. One method: inductive." Please don't hesitate to call us.

Finally, let me share my vision—it's the possibility of a new avenue of ministry for you, Beloved of God…

A new beginning—
An avenue of ministry—
A sense of doing something that has eternal value

These are three things I think are so important for you and for me. There's so much to learn, to know, to experience, to do—and we never want to lose sight of that. To do so would be to miss what God has for us. To fall short of the tremendous potential of our lives—a potential that is ours because we are His, because we are children of the Creator of the Universe, indwelt by His divine Spirit and given the mind of Christ. You and I, Beloved, are God's workmanship gifted by the Spirit of God and created in Christ Jesus unto good works that would absolutely stagger our minds if we were to see them before they ever happened.

And what has God put into your hands? What are you holding and reading right now? Is it an accident? A coincidence? No! You are holding a devotional study that first and foremost will be the beginning of a new depth of understanding about the sufficiency of God's grace day by day in every aspect of your life.

God is going to speak to you because through this book you are going to come face to face with the living Word of God—the Word that not only discerns the thoughts and intentions of your heart, but becomes the means of throwing His light on the direction your life is taking so you can know with absolute confidence where you are headed. If you listen to what He says—and by that I mean ordering your life accordingly—then there is, in a sense, a new beginning...of understanding, of purpose. A new level of Christlikeness is attained. You will be, as Paul would say, pressing on and attaining that for which Jesus Christ laid hold of you.

Which brings me to my next point—an avenue of ministry. What you have learned, God intends for you to share. I have a vision, and you, Beloved, are part of that vision. Our Lord's commission in Matthew 28 was that we make disciples of all men—that we teach them to observe all that He has commanded us. Acts 1 tells us that when we are saved and receive the Holy Spirit we become His witnesses—yet the question is often, "How?"

Here is the how. This "Lord" book contains truths every human being needs to know and to apply to his or her life. These are precepts for life; through them we will gain understanding and, as the psalmist says, "hate every false way" (Psalm 119:104). We hate it because it is false rather than true, and it is truth that sets us apart, sets us free.

So what is my vision for you, my friend? It is that you go to the Lord in prayer and ask Him to direct you to at least one other person—but preferably at least ten—and that you, along with them, study this book together. You may not be a teacher, but you can be the group's facilitator. You can take the questions you'll find at the end of each chapter and use them to stimulate a discussion among those whom the Lord has brought together in answer to your prayer. These are those who will be part of your crown of rejoicing in the presence of our Lord Jesus Christ. As you watch them learn and grow in the knowledge of God and of His Word, you will experience the humbling joy of knowing that you have been used of God. That what you have done has eternal value. That your life and God-given gifts have not been wasted. That your work will live on—that the grace of God poured out on you was not poured out in vain, for you have labored in the strength of His grace.

So as you facilitate a group using this book, you need to watch for and encourage others in your group to do as you have done—to take what they have learned and impart it to another as you did with them. Think of the multiplication that will happen! Do you realize, Beloved, that this is the way we can reach our neighborhoods, our communities, our nation, and beyond? Think of the transformation that will take place among all those people today who are so interested in "the spiritual" but won't step inside a church. Think—just think!—what is going to happen!

The time is now. The hour is short. Stop and pray right now and ask God what He would have you to do. He will show you, because He is God and because such prayers are in accordance with His will. As you step out and begin, just know that if you will step out in faith, God will give you an avenue of ministry, person by person or group by group, that will not only stagger your mind but absolutely delight your soul.

I cannot wait to hear what God does in and through you, my friend.

I FEEL SO UNWORTHY

Could someone who had two mental breakdowns and had attempted suicide three times ever be used of God?

Yes, because the grace of God has appeared to all men.

But after he knew God and had experienced the Spirit-filled life, if he then became depressed for over a year, could he ever again testify of the sufficiency of Jesus Christ?

Yes, because the grace of God has appeared to all men.

But could a man who had raped slaves, mocked the gospel, and tried to destroy the faith of others ever hope to know God, let alone be used of Him?

Yes, because there was grace…sufficient for all his sin.

But after he had believed in Christ Jesus, what if he was once again conquered by the lust of his eyes? What if he raped again? Could he ever hope to know the power of Christ upon his life, to know the benefits of His mercy?

Could he ever hope to be used by God? Or must he be condemned to a life without purpose?

No, for the grace of God has appeared to all men.

Neither William Cowper, the man who battled depression, nor John Newton, the rapist, would be denied renewed intimacy with God. God's grace covered all their sins and His grace would tie them to His love. Grace would forever anchor them within the veil of His presence.

William Cowper wrote: "There is a fountain filled with blood, drawn from Emmanuel's veins, and sinners plunged beneath that flood, lose all their guilty stains." His cry in the hymn "O' for a Closer Walk with God" would become the melodious plea of generations to follow. Cowper would become one of the major poets of England in the latter half of the eighteenth century.

Cowper's life touched generations as a result of God's amazing grace. He learned of God's grace through the testimony of the slave trader John Newton in the book *Out of the Depths*. Cowper was convinced that God's salvation could never reach him. But he began to believe otherwise through the friendship of the one who wrote, "Amazing grace how sweet the sound that saved a wretch like me." God would reach William Cowper with His grace. Grace, grace, marvelous grace coming down from the Father above. Amazing grace.

Grace is our subject of study. Grace that enables you to make it...no matter your need, no matter the circumstance, no matter the pull of the flesh or its weaknesses. The Lord is there with His grace, grace sufficient to make it!

For the next nine weeks this book needs to become your daily companion. Let it take you into the Scriptures. Meditate upon His Word. Do your assignments. Apply the truths of grace until they are absorbed into your soul. As you do, you'll soon find the grace of God softening the rough, parched areas of life.

— D A Y   T W O —

Have you despaired of pleasing God? Maybe you think you failed God. Maybe you didn't believe what He said. Or maybe you sinned, all the time knowing that what you were about to do was wrong.

Do you weep because you missed your opportunity of service? You made a choice—the wrong one—and now you are imprisoned in the consequences of your own way.

Or maybe you have taken account of who you are and what you have to offer, and you are firmly convinced that your life has little, if any, purpose to the Kingdom of God—let alone to the world.

You wonder, Why live? Why try? Why keep going when I will never go anywhere anyway?

Maybe none of these things bothers you. You have settled into your routine Christianity in a routine daily existence. At times it is mundane. But then you say, Considering who I am, there isn't much more I could expect anyway.

No, there really isn't much more to expect, *except for the grace of God.* As a matter of fact, if it weren't for the grace of God which has appeared to all men, we would all face defeat and despair.

As I write these words, I cannot help but wonder where you are, my friend. Have I struck a familiar chord? Why don't you answer the questions I have just asked? Write out how you would respond if we were sitting across the table from one another. To verbalize it will be good. Also, at the end of this study you can look back and see what has happened as a result of our time together spent studying what the Bible has to say on this topic.

O Beloved, if you are going to trust God in all things—
in times of failure,
in times of sin,
in times of weakness,
in times of sickness,
in times of confusion,
in times of distress,

in times of inadequacy,

in times of frustration—

then you need to understand and walk in the grace of God, which is available for everyone.

For the victorious Christian, the one who lives as more than a conqueror, grace is more than a theological term. Grace is a reality, a fact of life. It is by grace that one becomes a Christian, and it is by grace that one lives the Christian life.

Because prior to his conversion Paul persecuted and murdered Christians, he did not consider himself fit to be called an apostle. Yet, grace conquered his feelings. If anyone understood that grace covers our past and equips us for God's future, it was Paul! Listen to his words: "By the grace of God I am what I am, and His grace toward me did not prove vain; but I labored even more than all of them, yet not I, but the grace of God with me" (1 Corinthians 15:10).

In Paul's writing of those God-breathed words, we see that the whole of life is to be lived in the understanding and appropriation of the grace of God. Oh, how I pray that God will grant you this understanding and that He will anoint this writing to your good and His eternal glory.

– D A Y   T H R E E –

Nothing is more frustrating to me than an anonymous letter. It's a one-way conversation, and I can't respond. Little did I realize as I began reading the following anonymous letter that it was from a woman. When I got to the last desperate words, I knew I had no sure way of sharing with her the grace of God. And yet…

My heart is so heavy and my mind is weary. I am tired of the struggle. The one I have loved is dead. She took her life because of me. My sin is ever before me. How can God love or forgive me? When I read the Bible I feel so guilty and condemned!

Please warn your listeners to flee sexual sin. Tell them not even to think about it! I fell in love with my minister's wife, and she and I had an experience that drove her to suicide. I am so tempted to do the same! I can't live with what happened. Why did God allow her to take her life? Is she in hell? It would break my heart knowing this beautiful, godly woman missed out on heaven because of me.

I hate lesbianism and homosexuality...it's a perversion of what God intended. Yet God has given me a great deal of compassion for people caught up in the darkness of that lifestyle and has allowed me the privilege of ministering to many ensnared in this sin. But I wondered how I could ever minister to this woman. I knew if anyone ever needed to know of the grace of God, it was this anonymous soul.

Her letter went on to tell every detail of their night together. Why did she tell me all of the details? To defile or disgust me? No, I think it was because she was hurting desperately, and in her hurt was reliving every detail.

Her letter closed this way:

She called me everyday. Said she had to see me. I met her at a park one day. She lit up when she saw me. Came over to my car and sat down, reached over and kissed me smack on the lips!

"_____," I said, "What if someone should see us?" She didn't seem to care. Said she could only think of me, that she loved me and wanted me. She told me she couldn't live without me. When I told her that would be impossible and to get help, she left. I knew she needed help, but I didn't think she'd kill herself. I didn't take her seriously. How can I live with the responsibility of her death hanging over me?

Nobody else knows about this. Confessing it to her husband or children would be cruel and senseless. What can I do? How do I cope? Answer me with a booklet or a tape. Advertise it over your radio program. I'll hear about it. I can't identify myself.

Use this story to warn others. Please don't let this be in vain. My dream and fantasy became a reality!! It has ruined my life.

How I hurt for this woman! Truly she could live as a captive to the memory of the sin and the death of this woman unless she learned where and how to receive forgiveness and strength to go on with life. How I longed to get on the radio at that moment! Yet, the programs for "How Can I Live?" are prerecorded and sent to the stations weeks in advance.

I prayed. I planned what I would say over the air. Then a second letter came. I nearly died with joy when it came. Tears flooded my eyes, and I thought over and over, *What a great and marvelous God we serve. How wondrous are His ways.*

Since I wrote you last, a tremendous thing has happened. I found a class being taught which used one of your books—*Lord, I Need Grace to Make It.*

The Lord surely knew that class is what I needed. My heavy heart has lightened. I am no longer weary, and the best part of it all is that I have learned I don't have to struggle or be afraid of God. I have accepted His loving grace to cover my awful sin with my minister's wife. Even though she is gone and I may never see her again, I can have God's peace deep within my heart and life.

The joy of knowing that I am free in Christ and His grace on Calvary for me have made such a difference to my troubled mind. What relief He has already brought. I will continue on in this course to the end. Thank you for writing this book!

She signed it—"Your sister in Christ."

Now, dear student, can you understand why the phrase, "grace to you and peace" was far more than a familiar salutation often used by Paul in his epistles? In the Roman world where Paul moved, *grace* was a common Greek greeting, while among the Jewish community the greeting was *shalom* (peace). Combined in the context of Christianity, grace and peace took on a new meaning. When the grace of God appeared, bringing salvation to all men, it brought with it peace with God to a world alienated from Him by their sin (Titus 2:11-14).

The English transliteration of the Greek[1] word for grace is *charis*. In the Greek, the definition of the word was "unmerited favor." Paul seized this word with its secular meaning and expanded its definition to describe the unmerited favor which is given to all who come to God for salvation through His Son, the Lord Jesus Christ. Thus, we will see that God's grace carries with it an even deeper and richer definition than merely "unmerited favor."

The word *grace* appears 213 times in the New Testament. In the Old Testament no single word parallels the New Testament concept of grace. When the Old Testament was translated from Hebrew into Koine Greek, the Hebrew word *hen,* which meant "to find favor," was translated as *grace.*

In the *International Standard Bible Encyclopedia* we read, "Much nearer St. Paul's use of *charis* is *racon*...'acceptance.'"[2]

Richards, in his *Expository Dictionary of Bible Words,* suggests that the Hebrew word *hanan* ("to be gracious," "to be merciful") along with *hen* come closest to the New Testament concept of grace.[3] Although there is no Old Testament parallel for the New Testament concept of grace, we do see that the saints of old understood that God was always to be approached on the basis of grace and never on the basis of merit.

The Hebrew word *hanan* is used in Psalm 51 and is translated *gracious.* This is the psalm written by David after Nathan confronted him regarding his adulterous relationship with Bathsheba. Certainly David understood that he had no ground on which to approach God other than God's grace and mercy.

> Be gracious *[hanan]* to me, O God, according to Thy lovingkindness; according to the greatness of Thy compassion blot out my transgressions. Wash me thoroughly from my iniquity, and cleanse me from my sin....

Against Thee, Thee only, I have sinned, and done what is evil in Thy sight, so that Thou art justified when Thou dost speak, and blameless when Thou dost judge.... Create in me a clean heart, O God, and renew a steadfast spirit within me. (Psalm 51:1-2,4,10)

The grace of God was seen in the Old Testament too in His acceptance of a sacrificial animal to cover the sin of man.

O Beloved, do you understand, as David understood, that God alone can take care of your sin and cleanse your heart? It's all of grace! As you learn to walk in this grace, you will know His incredible peace.

Why don't you take a few minutes and write out a prayer to God. Pour out your heart to Him. Tell Him that you want to understand His grace, and then have faith to appropriate it.

Grace and peace to you, my friend.

— D A Y   F O U R —

Grace in its fullest sense is not seen in the Old Testament. I cannot help but think of John 1:17: "For the Law was given through Moses; grace and truth were realized through Jesus Christ." The New Testament is the declaration of the new covenant, the covenant of grace.

Although God has always granted salvation on the basis of grace, and grace alone, still grace was not realized until "the Word was made flesh, and dwelt among us, (and we beheld his glory, the glory as of the only begotten of the Father,) full of grace and truth" (John 1:14, KJV).

Until the Seed of Abraham and the Messenger of the New Covenant

—the Lord Jesus Christ—came, men were "kept in custody under the law, being shut up to the faith which was later to be revealed. Therefore the Law has become our tutor to lead us to Christ, that we may be justified by faith. But now that faith has come, we are no longer under a tutor" (Galatians 3:23-25).

Faith releases God's grace. Faith is the key that unlocks the door to the unmerited favor of God. And once that door is unlocked, we forever stand in the grace of God. "Therefore having been justified by faith, we have peace with God through our Lord Jesus Christ, through whom also we have obtained our introduction by faith into this grace in which we stand" (Romans 5:1-2).

These truths of Romans and Galatians are vital to a life of peace and victory! Many are living defeated lives because they do not realize what it means to live by grace—by grace alone.

I am not speaking of a perversion of grace which would lead to licentiousness. I am speaking of an understanding of grace which would release the power of God upon a life, a comprehension which would bring great peace and put a person in the undisturbed eye of the hurricane as they live more and more in the knowledge and experience of the grace of God.

Grace is more than unmerited favor. It is reality. By grace you live, by grace you please God, and by grace you are freed from religion and released into a relationship with your heavenly Father. Grace is always based on who He is and what He has done. Grace is never based on who you are apart from Him or on what you can do.

In light of what we've shared, stop and examine how you relate to your heavenly Father. What is the basis of your relationship with Him? Verbalize it by writing it down.

Have you ever really understood that there is nothing you can do to merit or earn God's favor?

Have you seen that "no good thing dwells within" you that would commend you for adoption as a child of God? What are you trusting for your salvation? And if you are sure that your salvation is all of grace, how then do you relate to God on a daily basis—on the basis of grace, or on the basis of the Law?

O Beloved, let's pray for one another, believing that our relationship with our Father will take on new depths through this study.

— D A Y   F I V E —

Grace is key to your relationship with God. The believer never comes to God on any basis other than grace. Therefore, if you are ever going to live by grace, you must understand—really understand—the grace of God which appeared and, in its appearing, brought salvation to all men. Once you have a clear, biblical understanding of grace, you will have a solid foundation upon which you can construct a life lived totally in the grace of God rather than one based on whether or not you deserve His blessing, His favor.

O Beloved, I want to pray for you now:

O Father, open the eyes of our understanding. Remove the veil of the Old Covenant so that we might see the glory of the New Covenant. I ask this for Your glory and for our peace…that it might release us into greater service for You. And I ask it in the name of the Messenger of the New Covenant, the Lord Jesus Christ. Amen and amen.

Now let me take you back to the Old Testament, right back to the beginning, to Genesis. Take a moment and read Genesis 3.

Let me ask you several questions that will be pertinent to our study. Write out the answers by observing carefully what the Word of God has to say. You need not go beyond the Word. Simply get your answers from what you read in Genesis 3.

1. What did the serpent say that Eve could be like if she would eat of the fruit of the tree of the knowledge of good and evil?

After Eve ate of the forbidden fruit, she gave it to Adam and he ate. Romans 5:12 tells us, "Therefore, just as through one man sin entered into the world, and death through sin, and so death spread to all men, because all sinned." Therefore, at the point of disobedience on the part of Adam and Eve, sin entered into the world.

2. Read Isaiah 53:6 and write it out.

3. Now, let's see how sin is defined in the Word. Look up the following verses and note what you learn about sin.
   a. 1 John 3:4

   b. James 4:17

   c. Romans 14:23

   d. Romans 3:23

4. In light of what the serpent told Eve, and after reading Isaiah 53:6, what would you say is the essence, or the root, of all sin?

Because Adam and Eve are the parents of all mankind, all mankind is born in sin. We see this truth expressed by David in Psalm 51:5: "Behold, I was brought forth in iniquity, and in sin my mother conceived me."

You and I are sinners! How can sinners ever hope to redeem themselves when it is their very nature to sin? People didn't have to teach you to lie, did they? Of course not! Rather, your parents had to encourage you, in one way or another, to tell the truth. Selflessness never comes naturally, does it, my friend? But selfishness does! And is obedience to God natural, or is it a challenge, a battle, from childhood on? And the wages of our sin? DEATH! What hope is there for us apart from the favor of God, apart from the gospel of grace? This gospel is first mentioned in Genesis 3. We will look at it tomorrow.

— DAY SIX —

Have you ever done something that you wanted to do, knowing full well that you shouldn't? At the time, the pleasure of it all might have made it seem worth it. You wanted your way, and you got it. But afterward—maybe immediately, maybe years later—how did you feel? Can you imagine how awful Adam and Eve felt once they ate of the fruit of the tree of the knowledge of good and evil?

Suddenly, rather than fellowshipping with God, they wanted to hide from Him. Sin immediately affected their relationship with God—and with each other.

Did you notice how Adam and Eve each passed the blame? Adam blamed Eve for what he had done. At the same time, he passed the blame on to God as he pointed out that it was God who had given him the woman who made him stumble!

Crucifixion is the only death that bruises the heel. Here is the first promise of the grace of God which would be realized in Jesus Christ! God made an unconditional promise in the face of man's willful disobedience. Grace, grace, amazing grace!

— D A Y   S E V E N —

Have you ever looked at circumstances and said, "No way! There is no human way out"? And there wasn't, short of some sort of divine intervention!

Once Adam had made his choice to follow in Satan's footsteps and exalt himself above God, to be as God, the die was cast. Adam and Eve would reproduce after their own kind. God made Adam "in the likeness of God," but sin distorted that likeness. So Adam became the father of those "in his own likeness, according to his image" (Genesis 5:1,3).

Redemption by man for man was impossible. Sinners cannot redeem themselves. Therefore, if God were ever to reconcile man to Himself, there would have to be a new Adam—a man born without sin. Only the grace of God could provide such a one: Jesus.

Are you beginning to see why Jesus had to be born of a virgin? Romans 5:12 says, "Therefore, just as through one man sin entered into the world, and death through sin, and so death spread to all men, because all sinned—"

Because we are born in sin, God moved in grace. He promised a Seed who would eventually triumph over the serpent of old, the devil (Revelation 12:11), by bruising his head. Oh, Satan would first bruise Christ's heel on Calvary. But the bruising of the heel would be temporary! Jesus would triumph over death! In the offering of the spotless, sinless Lamb of God, the just would die for the unjust. God's holiness would be satisfied. Thus, God would raise Jesus from the dead for our justification (Romans 4:25).

Not only was the promise given to Adam, but it was confirmed to Abraham on the day when Abraham believed God. God, in grace, counted

Abraham's faith as righteousness and made a covenant with him. This account is recorded for us in Genesis 15.

1. Read Genesis 15 and mark the following words (and/or their synonyms) distinctively from one another. You may want to use symbols to mark your words, or you may choose to use different colors, or a combination of both.

   Marking words that are key to the text—or that are key throughout the Word as a whole—will help you see those words instantly. It will also help you gather information as you will be able to track key subjects and quickly identify truths throughout Scripture.*

   a. offspring, seed, or descendants (You will want to always mark synonyms in the same way.)

   b. believe

   c. covenant

2. Now go back to see what you can note about each word since you have marked it. What does the chapter say about each? Under each word list what you see about it. As you review your marking and construct your list, ask yourself the "5 Ws and an H" (who, what, why, where, when, how) to see what you can find.

* See page 207 for section on marking your Bible.

3. Now let's look at one pertinent cross reference: Galatians 3:16. God wants us to see that once a covenant is made, it is never broken. In this verse Paul explains the relationship of the Old Covenant to the Abrahamic Covenant, which was a covenant of grace. Read Galatians 3:16 and answer the questions that follow.

"Now the promises were spoken to Abraham and to his seed. He does not say, 'And to seeds,' as referring to many, but rather to one, 'And to your seed,' that is, Christ."

a. According to this verse, when God promised Abraham a seed in Genesis 15:5 (translated *descendants* in the NASB), who was that Seed?

b. When Abraham was declared righteous, he was saved. Was he saved by faith or by works? Or to put it another way, by grace or by law?

4. How can you apply what you have learned this week to your relationship with God?

O Beloved, we have just begun! I can't tell you what liberty, what peace, what power awaits you—if you will but continue in this study. Remember, His power, His grace is perfected in our weakness. You will learn to glory in your weaknesses so that His power might rest upon you! What a contrast to what we hear from the world and its reasonings!

MEMORY VERSE

For the Law was given through Moses; grace and truth were realized through Jesus Christ.

JOHN 1:17

SMALL-GROUP DISCUSSION QUESTIONS

1. What was the root or the basis of the sin displayed by Adam and Eve's disobedience? What is the essence of all sin?
2. When Adam and Eve were confronted with their sin, what was their response?
3. What effect did their sin have on them? What did they do? Why didn't they respond to God's call?
4. What could Adam and Eve do to redeem themselves?
5. Explain what God had said would be the consequence of disobedience on Adam and Eve's part. Did He hold the line that He had drawn against which righteousness would be measured?
6. What was God's immediate response to their sin after the consequences were realized? Did He leave them in this condition?
7. What did God do to make provision for Adam and Eve? For you and me?
8. Why did God make a provision? What does this provision show us about our God?
9. We learned that grace was not seen in its fullest sense in the Old Testament. According to John 1:17, when was the grace of God truly realized?
10. Until the Son of God came, men were living under what covenant?
11. Yet how do we know that grace existed before the Law? What did God do for Adam and Eve?
12. What can you and I do to earn God's grace?

13. What is the key that releases us into the grace of God?
14. Once we have believed in Jesus Christ, accepting God's provision, what can remove us from that standing or position?
15. What is the key to your relationship with your heavenly Father?
16. Which covenant do you and I live under today?
17. Explain what living under that covenant means to us in our daily lives.
18. Upon what basis does God always grant salvation?
19. After your study this week, how would you define grace? What does that mean for your life?
20. What will change in your life as a result of your study this week?

chapter 2

MY SINS ARE EVER BEFORE ME...

J ohn and Charles Wesley knew the Scriptures. As a matter of fact, their lives were devoted to God. In the midst of a corrupt university, they had been the instigators of what came to be known as "The Holy Club." Those joining this group lived by strict rules of discipline as they strived to live in accordance with the letter of the law. These brothers rose at four in the morning for prayer and scripture reading and enlisted others to follow their same methods so that they, too, might live holy lives pleasing to God.

Yet, for all their religious exercises, for all their devotion to God, John and Charles Wesley were blind to the grace of God. They had never been "born again." Rather than embracing the free grace of God bought on Calvary, they agonized on Sinai, trying to fulfill the Law.

Once they climbed Sinai's jagged peaks, they thought they would find Jesus and His peace. But instead of coming into the brilliance of the Son, clouds of darkness and gloom surrounded them. God's voice seemed like the blast of a trumpet. Instead of bringing peace, the sound of His words brought fear and trembling. They understood well how Moses felt. The sight of Mount Sinai was "so terrible...that Moses said, 'I AM FULL OF FEAR and trembling'" (Hebrews 12:21).

You may wonder what I mean by "climbing Calvary and Sinai." I'm using a metaphor that I've learned from the Word of God. Let's take a few minutes to look at two key passages. If you are new to the study of the Word, don't let these verses throw you. Learn what you can. You may not understand the full implication of what these passages are teaching, but becoming familiar with them will give you a point of reference.

> For you have not come to a mountain that may be touched and to a blazing fire, and to darkness and gloom and whirlwind, and to the blast of a trumpet and the sound of words which sound was such that those who heard begged that no further word should be spoken to them. For they could not bear the command, "IF EVEN A BEAST TOUCHES THE MOUNTAIN, IT WILL BE STONED." And so terrible was the sight, that Moses said, "I AM FULL OF FEAR and trembling." But you have come to Mount Zion and to the city of the living God, the heavenly Jerusalem, and to myriads of angels, to the general assembly and church of the first-born who are enrolled in heaven, and to God, the Judge of all, and to the spirits of righteous men made perfect, and to Jesus, the mediator of a new covenant, and to the sprinkled blood, which speaks better than the blood of Abel. (Hebrews 12:18-24)

Read Exodus 19:1-2,10-25 and write out the name of the mountain so that you don't miss the point.

Although we are going to study Galatians 4:21-31 in depth later, I want you to acquaint yourself with its contents now.

> Tell me, you who want to be under law, do you not listen to the law? For it is written that Abraham had two sons, one by the bondwoman and one by the free woman. But the son by the bondwoman was born according to the flesh, and the son by the free woman through the promise. This is allegorically speaking: for these women are two covenants, one proceeding from Mount Sinai bearing children who are to be slaves; she is Hagar.

Now this Hagar is Mount Sinai in Arabia, and corresponds to the present Jerusalem, for she is in slavery with her children. But the Jerusalem above is free; she is our mother. For it is written, "REJOICE, BARREN WOMAN WHO DOES NOT BEAR; BREAK FORTH AND SHOUT, YOU WHO ARE NOT IN LABOR; FOR MORE ARE THE CHILDREN OF THE DESOLATE THAN OF THE ONE WHO HAS A HUSBAND." And you brethren, like Isaac, are children of promise. But as at that time he who was born according to the flesh persecuted him who was born according to the Spirit, so it is now also. But what does the Scripture say? "CAST OUT THE BONDWOMAN AND HER SON, FOR THE SON OF THE BONDWOMAN SHALL NOT BE AN HEIR WITH THE SON OF THE FREE WOMAN." So then, brethren, we are not children of a bondwoman, but of the free woman.

When John Wesley set sail with James Oglethorpe for America, he had one intent—the conversion of the Indians. Yet, it wasn't long before he returned to England a defeated, disillusioned man. He discovered he had been climbing the wrong mountain.

For years John and his brother, Charles, had totally missed the relationship of the Old Covenant given at Mount Sinai to the New Covenant given at Mount Calvary. But they were not alone. They were not the first, nor will they be the last, to fail to understand the relationship of these two covenants.

The Pharisees of Jesus' day were so taken with the Law that they were unable to recognize the grace of God which was so brilliantly demonstrated in their day. We shake our heads when we read of their blindness, yet many today walk around tapping the same white stick as they grope in the darkness and gloom of Mount Sinai's shadows. They have missed the narrow road of grace which leads to the light of eternal life.

And others come to Calvary for salvation but run back to Sinai, thinking they will find the path which will eventually make them acceptable to the One whom they call Father. They are miserable. Although they have been saved by grace, they do not know how to live in that grace.

Oh, may we see that the Christian life is *all* of grace. May we ever view Mount Sinai from the perspective of Mount Calvary. The view will bring great peace, even as it did to John and Charles Wesley when they finally understood the grace of God which had appeared to all men. Finally, they were saved!

– D A Y   T W O –

Have you ever wondered why the Old Covenant was instituted by God if salvation is all of grace and not of law?

Some of you may already know the answer. If you do, my friend, I know God will bless you and prepare you for the other awesome principles of life which will follow in our study as you review this truth. He will use this truth as a basis for our understanding of our need of grace so that we may respond correctly to conviction of sin and to the difficult circumstances of life.

Understanding the purpose of the Law will help you pray for and win your loved ones and others to the Lord. You will also see the importance of using the principles of the Law in teaching your children.

Four hundred thirty years after God made a covenant with Abraham, promising him the Seed—Jesus Christ—God made another covenant. This covenant was the covenant of the Law. Galatians 3:15-29 explains the purpose of the Law.

As you read, remember that grace and faith go together, as do law and works. Read the passage through the first time to become familiar with it. Then read it again and mark the following key words:

1. seed (and every reference to Jesus Christ)
2. covenant
3. law

4. promise

5. faith

◗ GALATIANS 3:15-29

15 Brethren, I speak in terms of human relations: even though it is only a man's covenant, yet when it has been ratified, no one sets it aside or adds conditions to it.

16 Now the promises were spoken to Abraham and to his seed. He does not say, "And to seeds," as referring to many, but rather to one, "And to your seed," that is, Christ.

17 What I am saying is this: the Law, which came four hundred and thirty years later, does not invalidate a covenant previously ratified by God, so as to nullify the promise.

18 For if the inheritance is based on law, it is no longer based on a promise; but God has granted it to Abraham by means of a promise.

19 Why the Law then? It was added because of transgressions, having been ordained through angels by the agency of a mediator, until the seed should come to whom the promise had been made.

20 Now a mediator is not for one party only; whereas God is only one.

21 Is the Law then contrary to the promises of God? May it never be! For if a law had been given which was able to impart life, then righteousness would indeed have been based on law.

22 But the Scripture has shut up all men under sin, that the promise by faith in Jesus Christ might be given to those who believe.

23 But before faith came, we were kept in custody under the law, being shut up to the faith which was later to be revealed.

24 Therefore the Law has become our tutor to lead us to Christ, that we may be justified by faith.

25 But now that faith has come, we are no longer under a tutor.

26 For you are all sons of God through faith in Christ Jesus.

27 For all of you who were baptized into Christ have clothed yourselves with Christ.

28 There is neither Jew nor Greek, there is neither slave nor free man, there is neither male nor female; for you are all one in Christ Jesus.

29 And if you belong to Christ, then you are Abraham's offspring, heirs according to promise.

In the space below list all you have learned from this passage regarding the Law. List the purpose of the Law and what it was never intended to do. If you understand this truth, you will know how to live in the grace of God on a daily basis.

Let me encourage you to persevere. As we progress, you will see how to live daily in the grace of God in practical ways. I realize you want to know how to cope with life immediately, if not sooner. However, my friend, if you are going to conquer life rather than be conquered by it, you must understand the Word of God. That will take some time, so be patient. Let's build truth by truth, absorbing each truth as we go.

— *D A Y   T H R E E* —

Have you ever taken a good look at the Ten Commandments? They really are pretty reasonable, aren't they? No murder, adultery, stealing, coveting. Anyone ought to be willing to keep them, especially if a person acknowledges the existence of God. The children of Israel thought so when Moses gave them God's commandments.

> Then Moses came and recounted to the people all the words of the LORD and all the ordinances; and all the people answered with one voice, and said, "All the words which the LORD has spoken we will do!" And Moses wrote down all the words of the LORD. Then he arose early in the morning, and built an altar at the foot of the mountain with twelve pillars for the twelve tribes of Israel. And he sent young men of the sons of Israel, and they offered burnt offerings and sacrificed young bulls as peace offerings to the LORD. And Moses took half of the blood and put it in basins, and the other half of the blood he sprinkled on the altar. Then he took the book of the covenant and read it in the hearing of the people; and they said, "All that the LORD has spoken we will do, and we will be obedient!" So Moses took the blood and sprinkled it on the people, and said, "Behold the blood of the covenant, which the LORD has made with you in accordance with all these words." (Exodus 24:3-8)

The children of Israel obviously found God's commandments reasonable. They intended to keep them. But they didn't!

And what about you? Have you found God's commandments keep-able? Have you always loved God? Have you ever put anything in His rightful place, making an idol of that person or thing? Have you always honored your father and mother? Have you ever committed adultery or murder—if not physically, then mentally? Have you ever wanted something that belonged to somebody else?

When you broke any of the Ten Commandments, how did you handle it? What did you do to make it right with God? Write your answer here.

What did you write, Beloved? When your foot slipped and you trans-gressed God's holy Law, and you found yourself clutching the slippery rock, hanging on for dear life, did you look to the grace of God to rescue you? Or did you pull yourself up, determined to keep on trying to please God?

— D A Y   F O U R —

The Law was never intended to make a man or woman righteous, whether he or she was a lost person or a saved person. If you and I could remember this truth, it would forever cast us upon His grace. Grace would become the key that would unlock a life of greater peace, trust, confidence, and intimacy with our heavenly Father and His Son as we walk hand in hand with the Spirit of grace.

Do you remember what you read in Galatians 3? The Law was not given to make us righteous. If the Law could sanctify us, we would not need Jesus Christ and the grace which He brings. The Law was added to the promise given to Abraham—the promise of the coming of the Seed, Jesus Christ—"because of transgressions." (Or it could be translated "for the sake of defining transgressions.") In other words, the Law was given in order to show us our sin.

When the children of Israel said they would keep the Law—that all God had commanded they would obey—they didn't begin to recognize their inability to keep the Law. They didn't understand their own power-lessness to be righteous. The Law showed them how a righteous man would live. However, they didn't see their own unrighteousness.

Can you relate? It's hard to see our own inability to be righteous, isn't it? We have a high estimation of man. We think we can do it on our own. If we can't, at least we have to try! Or we have a wrong understanding of God. We think He won't do what we desperately need Him to do, espe-cially if we don't do our share. We try, at least, to combine our little bit of righteousness and power with His. We think we have to do our part to make ourselves a little more acceptable, don't we? I have had to deal with this feeling, and I am sure you probably have also. Instead we need to cast ourselves totally upon the grace of God.

Several months ago I received a letter from a woman who had just completed our Precept Upon Precept Bible study course on Covenant. This letter illustrates the freedom that a correct understanding of grace brings.

I don't know how to share with you what God has done in my life through this study of Covenant, so I will simply share my prayer of rejoicing in our Lord.

My dear Father, thank you for showing me the wrong course I was taking. I had put myself under the Law and I was living each day under bondage, trying to reach some impossible, unattainable perfection or spiritual accomplishment. I was seeking to please you with my works rather than by faith. I was miserable because I saw I constantly failed, fell short, didn't measure up. I felt You not as a loving Father, not as a kind, caring Savior, not as my Beloved, but as one impossible to please, and yet

I wore myself out trying to please you, trying to earn or keep or regain your approval.

I began by your Spirit…when you picked me up and brought me to salvation, not through anything I had done, or even any desire or seeking on my part to know You. You chose me, drew me to yourself, showed me your love. At first I knew nothing of fleshly works. My salvation was so obviously completely of you. I knew only resting, trusting, rejoicing in your love. As the years went by I became more and more wrapped up in myself and trying to please you; not realizing (or remembering) how completely I was already accepted in Christ, how utterly futile [it was] to try to please you by any works of my own, not understanding the power of your Spirit within me to cause me to fear you, to cause me to walk in a way that pleased you. I was so afraid of making a mistake.

When I was under the Law I was powerless and ineffective as a witness. I kept thinking, "Why would anyone want this?" Anyone looking at me would not want what I had. I was miserable. But now! Now the love of Jesus can flow through me once again and I can walk in confidence rather than fear.

Were there things in my friend's letter that you related to? Underline them and then ask God to open your eyes that you might understand His grace.

— D A Y   F I V E —

The kingdom of Judah was on the brink of judgment. They had broken God's covenant and had refused to repent. The Babylonians had already besieged Jerusalem. Then came the word of the Lord to Jeremiah. It would eventually apply to all mankind. Listen:

"Behold, days are coming," declares the LORD, "when I will make a new covenant with the house of Israel and with the house of Judah, not like the covenant which I made with their fathers in the day I took them by the hand to bring them out of the land of Egypt, My covenant which they broke, although I was a husband to them," declares the LORD. "But this is the covenant which I will make with the house of Israel after those days," declares the LORD, "I will put My law within them, and on their heart I will write it; and I will be their God, and they shall be My people. And they shall not teach again, each man his neighbor and each man his brother, saying, 'Know the LORD,' for they shall all know Me, from the least of them to the greatest of them," declares the LORD, "for I will forgive their iniquity, and their sin I will remember no more." (Jeremiah 31:31-34)

1. What covenant did they break?

2. How would this New Covenant differ from the Old Covenant as far as the law of God was concerned?

3. According to what you have just read in Jeremiah, list below the other benefits that this New Covenant would bring.

4. From reading this passage, who would bring about all of this—the LORD or the people?

The Old Covenant, the Law, is referred to by Paul as a "ministry of death, in letters engraved on stones" (2 Corinthians 3:7) and as a "ministry of condemnation" (2 Corinthians 3:9). And that, Beloved, is what you will continually live under until you learn to live in the light of the grace of God. It is amazing how many Christians don't understand what it is to live in the grace of God, in the "ministry of the Spirit" (2 Corinthians 3:8), experiencing God's blessing and help rather than living under condemnation.

As you learn, you are going to be able to say with Paul that God's grace was not given to you in vain. A lack of understanding of the grace of God keeps many people from living lives that have eternal significance.

Do you ever say, "But I am so ordinary. God could never use me! Look at me! Look at my life! Look at my failures! Look at my inadequacies!"?

Stop looking at yourself, friend. Look at the grace of God which has appeared to *all.*

– D A Y   S I X –

Have you ever feared that someday you might turn your back and deny you ever knew the Lord Jesus Christ? I have. I knew deep in my heart that it was something I never wanted to do, but I also understood how deceptive my heart is.

Have you ever wondered if God would someday walk away from you, abandoning you, leaving you alone?

Thoughts like this could keep a person from taking a bold stand for the Lord, couldn't they? We think, *What if God abandons me once I give myself to Him?* Or we have a tendency to look at our own weaknesses and frailties and think, *I can't, God. Get someone else.*

However, once we understand the promises of the New Covenant, we see that all things are possible to the one who believes because He will never leave us nor forsake us. We can boldly say, "THE LORD IS MY HELPER" (Hebrews 13:5-6).

There are still other passages in the Old Testament about the New Covenant that I want you to see. You should know the whole counsel of God regarding the grace of God! Therefore, let me take you today to Jeremiah 32 and Ezekiel 36.

In Jeremiah 32:38-40, we gain an even deeper understanding of what it means to belong to God, to become His people through the New Covenant of grace. Let's take a good look at this passage. You will need to answer some questions so that you see truth for yourself. This process will help you remember these truths! Read the verses from Jeremiah aloud. It will make a difference.

> And they shall be My people, and I will be their God; and I will give them one heart and one way, that they may fear Me always, for their own good, and for the good of their children after them. And I will make an everlasting covenant with them that I will not turn away from them, to do them good; and I will put the fear of Me in their hearts so that they will not turn away from Me. (Jeremiah 32:38-40)

1. Who is making the promises in these verses?

2. List the specific things God promises.

3. According to this promise, could you—would you—ever turn away from God? Why?

4. How does what you've just seen compare with what you studied yesterday in Jeremiah 31?

5. How long is this covenant in effect? How do you know?

Now let's go to Ezekiel 36:26-27. Read it aloud.

Moreover, I will give you a new heart and put a new spirit within you; and I will remove the heart of stone from your flesh and give you a heart of flesh. And I will put My Spirit within you and cause you to walk in My statutes, and you will be careful to observe My ordinances.

1. According to this passage, who makes every provision needed for the covenant?

2. What is done that makes a person different?

3. How does this parallel the verses from Jeremiah 31 and 32 that you looked at?

4. God's statutes and ordinances are God's Law. According to this promise in the New Covenant, what are the recipients of this covenant able to do?

Finally, suppose you believed all that you have just read regarding the New Covenant. On the basis of that belief, what have you seen and learned that would enable you to serve God in confidence? How would these truths affect your relationship with God the Father and His Son, the Lord Jesus Christ? Write out your insights below.

— D A Y   S E V E N —

The Law can't change you. It only presents God's requirements for pleasing Him. It can't transform your heart, even a heart that desires to please God, because our hearts are deceitful and desperately wicked.

Self is at the core of every human heart. Peel off all of the layers around the core—some which seem to be good—and you will see that all of it grew out of self. If you are to be righteous from the inside out, you must have a new heart and receive forgiveness for the sins which you have committed.

The New Covenant brings forgiveness and a new heart. What you or I cannot do, God can do. The New Covenant grants us forgiveness of sins. So glorious is this forgiveness that God remembers the sins no more! Plus, to deal with the ever-present problem of slavery to sin, God removes our heart of stone and gives us a new heart, a heart of flesh. And not only that, He puts His Spirit within us. Whereas we were without the Spirit of God because of our identification with Adam, now, through the New Covenant, God in mercy saves us "not on the basis of deeds which we have done in righteousness, but according to His mercy, by the washing of regeneration and renewing by the Holy Spirit, whom He poured out upon us richly through Jesus Christ our Savior" (Titus 3:5-6).

It is the presence of the indwelling Holy Spirit that enables us to keep God's statutes and ordinances. Thus, when we walk by the Spirit, we do not carry out the desires of the flesh (Galatians 5:16). And it is the Spirit within which causes us to fear Him (fear means "to have a reverential respect"). It is the Spirit who keeps us from turning away from Him.

It is grace, grace, grace. God does it all. Ours is only to believe. Even the faith to believe is of grace. It is all of grace.

It is by grace that we are saved.

It is by grace that we know Him intimately.

It is by grace that we live day by day.

By grace we deal with the traumas of life.

By grace we serve God.

By grace we please God. By grace we deal with our sins when we do not walk by the Spirit but yield to the flesh.

By grace, and grace alone, we approach God and receive the things which we need—whether spiritual, emotional, or physical.

Through the obedience of faith, we lay hold of the grace of God, believing God and walking in obedience to Him, no matter what.

O Beloved, go to the Lord in prayer. Thank Him for all that is yours through the New Covenant.

MEMORY VERSE

Therefore having been justified by faith, we have peace with God through our Lord Jesus Christ, through whom also we have obtained our introduction by faith into this grace in which we stand; and we exult in hope of the glory of God.

ROMANS 5:1-2

SMALL-GROUP DISCUSSION QUESTIONS

In week one we saw that God created us and set boundaries for us to live by. These boundaries were not put in place to make us unhappy or to stifle us in any way. They were established for our good, for our protection.

We saw that our disobedience to the standard which God had set brought death and separation from God. Then we saw how God, in His great graciousness, reached over that line and made provision for us to be reconciled to Him.

We looked at the fact that faith is the key that unlocks the grace of God. And we learned it is by grace through faith that we are saved, and it is by grace through faith that we live a victorious Christian life day by day.

1. Why did God ever institute the Old Covenant?
2. What did you learn this week about the Law? What was it never intended to do?
3. When the Law does its job in our lives and exposes our sin, where can we turn?
4. From what you saw in the passage from Jeremiah 31, what was the main difference between the Old Covenant and the New Covenant of which God spoke here?
5. You also read about this New Covenant in a passage from Jeremiah 32. How long does the New Covenant last? How do you know?

6. Once you have entered into this New Covenant, will you ever turn and walk away from God permanently? Why?

7. In Ezekiel 36, what did you learn that we are given as we enter into the New Covenant?

8. What does God do that will cause us to walk in His ways?

9. As far as God is concerned, what happens to our sin when we enter into the New Covenant?

10. From the passages you studied, what enables us to keep the Law?

11. How do we enter into this New Covenant? What is our responsibility in order to enter? Where do we receive the ability to do that?

12. At this point, share what you see as the differences between the two covenants.

13. Upon which covenant is your daily relationship with your Father based?

14. Upon which mountain do you stand in times of failure, in times of need, in times of hopelessness? Why?

15. Do you see that to live under the Old Covenant is not to accept the graciousness of your heavenly Father who has made a far better way for you?

16. What is your response? What will change in your life today and in the days to come as a result of the grace of God that has been poured out to all men?

HOW CAN I KEEP
YOUR HOLY LAWS?

I'm always touched by the mail I receive. Sometimes I hurt, sometimes I rejoice, and sometimes I get angry. Angry, not because they are saying something I don't like, but angry because of the awful things people can do to one another, or because of the horrible situations they get themselves into.

Just recently I unfolded a letter written on pages from a yellow legal pad. The printing on this handwritten note was large, slanted, and almost energetic. Immediately, and naturally, my heart was touched, for the first two words were "Dearest Kay." It was from a young man. He had spent ten of his twenty-eight years behind bars. He had been out for four months at the time the letter was written.

A criminal and a drug addict, he said that the local district attorney had at one time described him as an "anti-social, sociopathic, paranoid-schizophrenic, homicidal maniac with tendencies toward suicidal actions." The district attorney wanted him to get the maximum sentence on a murder charge.

Like many today he was a young man raised with no knowledge of God nor of His Word. There were no moral restraints to keep him from destroying himself or others. He lived without any fear of God because he had no knowledge of God. Untaught in the Scriptures, he had nothing stored in his memory bank to restrain him when he was tempted to do whatever pleased him. He said he was dangerous because he did not care if he died.

After having been cut up in gang wars and overdosing on heroin, cocaine, and other destructive drugs, he said, "If, dear lady, you ever see me in person you will have seen a physical miracle that the Lord God Almighty has not only saved, but healed." At one time he was in the intensive care unit on heart, kidney, lung, and other machines because a rival gang member had put sulfuric acid in his vodka and rum. By all rights he should have died. Instead, God brought him to Himself, and he understood the grace of God that has appeared to all men…even to those who from the beginning of their lives heard nothing about God or His Son.

Such was not the case with John Newton. He had no excuse for his blasphemous infidelity. John's father was often at sea. His mother, Elizabeth, sick with tuberculosis, spent many of her days on the couch instructing John in the things of God. At age four he could read any book. He was carefully taught passages of Scripture, catechisms, hymns, and poems. When he was six, his mother began to teach him Latin.

John's father wanted his son to follow him to sea. Yet, Elizabeth prayed that John would someday become a preacher. God, in His grace and in His time, answered Elizabeth's prayer. But that answer did not come until John had experienced the depths of sin—sin that made him a slave of his raw passions as he rebelled against the knowledge of God.

Elizabeth Newton died when John was six. At eleven he went to sea with his father. It seemed as if his father would get his way. And for a while he did.

When he was seventeen, John met Polly Catlett, the daughter of the family who had nursed his mother until her death. Although Polly was thirteen, he fell in love with her. But even John's love for Polly would not keep him from raping the black women chained in the hold of the slave ships which he sailed. While he used women for his pleasure, Satan was using John for his.

Later he would give testimony: "I rejoiced…that I now might be as abandoned as I pleased, without any restraint…. I not only sinned with a high hand myself but made it my study to tempt and seduce others upon every occasion."[1]

At the age of twenty-one, John returned from Africa to England and to Polly on a voyage which would take twelve months:

John fouled the ship with his presence. His filthy language shocked even the roughest of the sailors. If any of the crew had a semblance of Christian belief, John sought to shred it. He mocked the gospel and derided Jesus Christ. When in a drunken stupor he nearly plunged overboard into the Atlantic, the ship's captain wondered if maybe John was a Jonah who should be thrown to the whales in order to preserve the lives of the other crew members.

Then one evening as the ship began heading north, John picked up a translation of Thomas à Kempis's *The Imitation of Christ* and read the words, "Life is of short and uncertain continuance…. Today the man is vigorous…and tomorrow he is cut down, withered and gone." The words clung to him, no matter how much he tried to shrug them off.

That night a fierce storm struck. John heard the screams of a sailor as he lost his life. "The ship is sinking," voices shouted in the dark. John, along with the others, manned the pumps and plugged the leaks. For hours they labored, seeking to save their lives and salvage what remained of the ship.

Exhausted by his toils and despairing that there was anything else he could do, John muttered, "If this will not do, the Lord have mercy on us." Then he thought about what he had said. It startled him. When he had nowhere else to turn, he had actually acknowledged God and had asked for mercy.[2]

O Beloved, have you ever despaired of being a godly person because of your upbringing? Do you feel that because you had a godly upbringing but turned away in rebellion there is no real forgiveness for you? Or do you feel that because you had no exposure to the things of God and have so sown a life of sin you'll never be able to be what you could have been? Write out what's in your heart. As you do, briefly describe your upbringing. We'll continue our discussion tomorrow.

$-$ D A Y   T W O $-$

Let me continue the account of John Newton's salvation as told by William Petersen in his insightful book *Johann Sebastian Bach Had a Wife*. Petersen has several wonderful books like this that you will want to buy and read because they will so encourage you in your walk with the Lord. Next to the Bible, biographies of the heroes of the faith have been the thing the Lord has used the most in calling me to a godly walk with Him. In this book I am using stories from several so you can see examples of men who sailed life's rough waters, arriving home safely.

> [The day after the storm] no one else knew what was going on in John's mind. For most of the day he stood at the helm of the ship, exhausted from manning the pumps the night before and steering as best he could. He mused over the question whether such a profane sinner as he could obtain mercy from God. When he tried to recall Scripture verses that spoke of pardon and forgiveness, all that came to his mind were passages that reminded him of judgment. "I waited with fear and impatience to receive my inevitable doom."
>
> Gradually, however, his thoughts turned to Jesus Christ and to the Crucifixion. He recalled that Jesus Christ did not die for his own sins; Jesus died for the sins of others. The only question that John now had was whether he had gone too far to be included with the "others."

Those eleven hours at the helm were decisive hours for John. Later he wrote, "March 21 is a day to be remembered by me. I have never suffered it to pass wholly unnoticed since the year 1748." He was not yet twenty-three.

As the ship struggled back to England, John began reading the New Testament and was especially heartened by the story of the prodigal son. "The prodigal had never been so exemplified as by myself."

There was no euphoria, no delirious heights of joy as he entered the kingdom. He was still wrestling, trying to understand, trying to see how he fit into God's scheme of mercy. But there was no doubt in his mind that God had hold of him. "I see no reason why the Lord singled me out for mercy...unless it was to show, by one astonishing instance, that with him 'nothing is impossible.'"

[John Newton had] wallowed through a muck of experiences in Africa. He had been wracked with disease, had been wasted by near starvation, and had participated in every type of sordid activity imaginable. He had kept a native mistress. Death had seemed commonplace; life had been cheapened; cruelty, brutality, and rape were daily occurrences. And he had gone from the depths of despair and contemplation of suicide to a redeeming relationship with God through Jesus Christ.[3]

O Beloved, where are you right now? Do you think there is no way out of the mess you are in? Out of the despair that is holding you captive? Do you seem to be caught in the quicksand of sin where struggling only seems to take you deeper in the mire of it all?

Take a few minutes and write out what you are struggling with and what you have done to try to help yourself.

Do you remember what Paul wrote in Romans 7? Listen to it again. As you read it, mark every reference to *Law* and in another distinctive way mark every reference to *sin*.

▶ ROMANS 7:14-25

14 For we know that the Law is spiritual; but I am of flesh, sold into bondage to sin.

15 For that which I am doing, I do not understand; for I am not practicing what I would like to do, but I am doing the very thing I hate.

16 But if I do the very thing I do not wish to do, I agree with the Law, confessing that it is good.

17 So now, no longer am I the one doing it, but sin which indwells me.

18 For I know that nothing good dwells in me, that is, in my flesh; for the wishing is present in me, but the doing of the good is not.

19 For the good that I wish, I do not do; but I practice the very evil that I do not wish.

20 But if I am doing the very thing I do not wish, I am no longer the one doing it, but sin which dwells in me.

21 I find then the principle that evil is present in me, the one who wishes to do good.

22 For I joyfully concur with the law of God in the inner man,

23 but I see a different law in the members of my body, waging war

against the law of my mind, and making me a prisoner of the law of sin which is in my members.

24 Wretched man that I am! Who will set me free from the body of this death?

25 Thanks be to God through Jesus Christ our Lord!

Who is presented as the One who can set you free?

Do you see that there is a way out? As you are caught in the quicksand of sin where struggling seems only to take you deeper in the mire, do you see that grace, only grace, can rescue you? Have you laid hold of it? If not, you will drown in your iniquity. Nothing can pull you out except the grace of God.

— D A Y   T H R E E —

It was the Word that Elizabeth Newton so faithfully sowed in John's heart that God used to bring John face to face with the grace of God. Therefore, it is vital that we stop at this point and see just how God uses the Law to bring men and women to faith in Jesus Christ.

The clearest and most thorough explanation of the gospel is found in the book of Romans. In Romans 1:16–3:20, Paul establishes the fact that all, both Jews and Gentiles, are under sin. Paul concludes by showing the purpose of the Law. Then he wants us to see how God saved us "as a gift by His grace" apart from the Law (Romans 3:24).

1. Turn to Romans 3:19-20 in your Bible, and read these verses carefully. Mark them in some way so that you can find them whenever you are looking for them.

2. Write out Romans 3:20. Read it aloud once you've written it out. You should memorize this verse.

3. What two things do you learn regarding the Law in Romans 3:20?

4. How does what you see in Romans 3:20 compare with Galatians 3:19?

Stop and think. How did you see your need of a Savior?

— *D A Y   F O U R* —

When my friend Carol went shopping that Saturday afternoon, little did she realize what part she would play in the chain of events God would use to bring Thomas Mitchell to Himself.

On February 26, 1977, Thomas Mitchell walked into a dress shop in downtown Chattanooga, wielded a knife, and threatened the lives of the salesladies if they got up from the floor where he had demanded they lie facedown. Not satisfied with the money in the cash register, he went into the dressing rooms to see whom he could rob.

Carol was trying on a dress. She was totally unaware of what had just taken place. Now she was face to face with a man who was telling her to take off all her clothes and lie down on the floor. Carol thought he was going to rape her. She refused to follow his instructions. Suddenly she felt the sharp edge of Thomas's knife slide down her cheek.

That was enough! She had just been taught in our Tuesday morning Bible class that, like Joshua, we are to be strong and courageous. In Carol's usual calm and gentle voice, she said, "In the name of Jesus Christ, I command you to leave me alone."

Suddenly Thomas Mitchell felt the presence of something very strong and powerful. "My physical being," as he would later write, "was unable to function temporarily. Chills went down my back."

Thomas staggered from the dressing room, followed by Carol, saying, "Praise the Lord! Praise the Lord!"

Thomas was captured and incarcerated again. He had already been convicted of murdering two people. There seemed no hope for him. Often he contemplated suicide. Yet, something restrained him. In isolation, with only a small New Testament, he found himself reliving over and over the events of February 26.

Almost a year later, in January 1978, God brought Thomas to Himself. I got to tell Carol the good news! How she wept! She had faithfully beseeched the Lord to save him.

Soon after his conversion, Thomas sat down and wrote a long letter to Carol, telling her how God had used that event in the dress shop to bring him to salvation. Although Thomas will be in prison for the rest of his life, he writes, "My soul will forever be free." In all these years of living in prison, Thomas has demonstrated the power of grace to save to the uttermost.

When I came to this section of the book—grace and the Law—I could not help but remember something Thomas shared with Carol. I'll never forget it! Although Thomas blames no one but himself for his life of crime, he remembers how his mother saved him from the consequences of his first misdemeanor at the age of fourteen. Although he was one of fifteen children, she always came to his defense and got him out of trouble. As a teenager, he always got away with whatever he did. He never paid the consequences. "I came to feel that someone would always get me out. I believe that was one of the reasons I ended up in prison for life."

I couldn't help but think of how God brings us to Himself and to a life of righteousness. God puts restraints on us through the Law. The Law cannot save us, but it can restrain us from messing up our lives. It is good to know and remember the purpose of the Law, especially if you are raising children or if you have input into the lives of your nieces, nephews, or grandchildren.

A knowledge of God's Law serves three purposes. First, *the Law sets before us the righteous standards of God.* We see what it is to live righteously, in a way that pleases God. "The Law is holy, and the commandment is holy and righteous and good" (Romans 7:12). The Law shows us what God expects from us.

The problem is not the Law. We are the problem! We are unholy, unrighteous, ungodly sinners. So even when we try to live according to the Law, we will always break it in one way or another.

Thus, we come to the second purpose of the Law: *By the Law is the knowledge of sin.* When we know what God expects and don't live up to it, we see our sin. As you teach your children the commandments of God, they will see that they fall short of God's standard. This understanding brings the knowledge of sin. It is sinners who need a Savior. Jesus came not to call the righteous, but sinners, to repentance.

John Newton's knowledge of the commandments of God and the consequences of his sin brought him to the grace of God.

The Law also serves a third purpose, if it is heeded. *It serves as a tutor, a schoolmaster to bring us to Christ.* If John Newton had listened to his mother and honored all that she stood for and taught him, it would have saved him much grief and remorse. He failed to allow the Law to be his schoolmaster.

As you bring up your children under the Law of God, you are putting them under a schoolmaster that will show them their need for the grace of God. If they heed the Law, it will serve as a guard against a life of blatant sin and the bitter consequences that come from transgressing God's holy commandments.

Many are suffering because they have failed to instruct their children in the Law of the Lord. Parents have neglected the Word of God, and children have reaped the consequences!

If your children know the Law and obey it, they will not need to worry about the guilt of immorality, murder, stealing, coveting, etc. They will honor you and your neighbors. They will not get swept away by witchcraft or the Eastern religions. Although they can never live perfectly, they can be kept from the pollution of a life of blatant sin.

If parents don't neglect the Word of God, but children don't follow what their parents have taught and modeled for them by their lifestyle, the total responsibility will fall on the child. Remember, Beloved, each one of us is individually accountable to God. Only God can bring your child to Himself.

Teach your children the difference between right and wrong—the Law—but keep telling them of the grace of God that can be theirs through Jesus Christ and the New Covenant. Pray diligently for them. Live out your Christianity before them. Then know that you did all you could do. The rest is up to God…and there you must rest. Certainly the lesson seen in John Newton's life is "where sin increased, grace abounded all the more" (Romans 5:20).

The seed sown by Elizabeth in John's life eventually brought him to Jesus Christ and to the grace of God. Those six years God gave her with her son were not wasted.

We have talked much about the Law, but let's take a few minutes to define it before we call it a day.

1. From memory, list below the essence of the Ten Commandments. Don't look in your Bible! This may be a humbling experience, but it will be good for you. Don't be concerned about order; simply see how many you can remember.

2. Now look up Exodus 20 in your Bible and fill in any commandment you missed.

3. The Ten Commandments basically fall into two categories.
   a. Look up Matthew 22:36-40 and note these categories below.

   b. Now look up Romans 13:8-10. What one thing can we do that will fulfill the Law? How does it do this? To answer this last question, remember what the Ten Commandments are.

4. Finally, my friend, if you have children or have influence in the life of a child, think of how you can use the Ten Commandments in teaching them to live. Write out your insights below.

— D A Y   F I V E —

Many times our witness for Jesus Christ lacks power because we don't allow the Law of God to convict sinners of their sin. We forget that Jesus Christ came into the world to save sinners!

Salvation is not merely salvation from hell and eternal condemnation. Hell and eternal condemnation are the consequences of sin. When one is saved, one is saved from the power of sin.

Yet people are told that they need to get saved so that they won't go to hell. It is true that if they are saved, they will never taste eternal death. They will never spend eternity in the lake of fire where the worm doesn't die and the fire isn't quenched. However, the reason people who are saved don't go to hell is because the lake of fire is the *consequence* of sin.

When we are saved, we are saved from *sin*. We are freed from sin's penalty or consequences (eternal condemnation in the lake of fire), from sin's power, and from sin's presence. One day we will leave this sinful world and go to be with the Father, where there is no sin.

Do you see my point? When we present salvation as merely an escape from eternal judgment, we have a tendency to deal lightly with the issue of sin. And when we deal lightly with sin, we weaken the grace of God— the unearned, undeserved, unmerited favor of God—which is poured out on us while we are ungodly, helpless sinners who are enemies of God.

That undeserved, unearned, unmerited favor of God is not passive. Grace delivers us from sin's penalty and sin's reigning power. Therefore, when we communicate the gospel, we need to make certain that people see and understand the following truths:

1. We are sinners. A person must fully realize that he has chosen to walk his own way, to be his own god, and that in the process has violated the holy commandments of God. He must see that he has known to do good, yet has not done it. He has not walked by faith—listening to, believing, and obeying God's Word. This is where the Law comes

in, for by the Law is the knowledge of sin. Look up Romans 3:9-18, and read it carefully. What is this passage saying?

2. The just consequence of sin will be eternal separation from God and eternal condemnation in the lake of fire. Read Revelation 20:11-15 and ask the "5 Ws and a H": who, what, when, where, why, and how. For example, who is going to be where? When? Why? What will happen? How will they be judged? Note what you learn below.

3. Jesus Christ came to save men and women from their sins. Look up Matthew 1:21 and 1 Timothy 1:15 and write these verses out. Jesus did this by becoming a man and by dying in our place "that by the grace of God He might taste death for everyone" (Hebrews 2:9).

   I want to restate something to be certain that you haven't missed it. Salvation is salvation from sin; the lake of fire is a consequence of our sin. When our sin is taken care of, we don't experience its consequence. Think about it, my friend.

   Will you ask God to lead you to someone with whom you might share all that you are learning, someone who needs the Lord Jesus Christ?

53

right in the middle of Paul's
ght want to read the entire

s is God and that He is to
will be expected to honor
acknowledge His rightful
n. When Adam and Eve
chose to be like God, to

ming to salvation is no
t to God and to God's
es not make us lawless;

teous. Only God can
faith. If a person will
He is who He says He
been saved through
od; not as a result of
workmanship, cre-
repared beforehand,
Underline the part

d them. Then, ask
the gospel of grace
spel. Don't worry
ome sow...others
:6-8).

d the
f God
are in
version
ent, and
ertain to

see the fol-

upon Jesus.
veness of sins
5:21, mark it

n't it fill you with

change of mind evi-
following verses on
verse is saying.

c. Acts 26:15-20 (Note: These verses are
   testimony before Agrippa, so you mi;
   testimony.)

Repentance causes a person to see that Jesu
be honored as God. As children of God, we
God as God rather than being our own gods! To
place as God is to be willing to be saved from s
chose to disobey God in the garden of Eden, the
be their own god.

Salvation reverses this choice. A person co
longer a law unto himself but is willing to subm
holy commandments. Why? Because salvation do
it makes us righteous.

3. People can't change their lives and become rig!
   transform man, and He does it by grace throug!
   believe on the Lord Jesus Christ, believing that I
   is, God will do the rest. "For by grace you have
   faith; and that not of yourselves, it is the gift of C
   works, that no one should boast. For we are Hi
   ated in Christ Jesus for good works, which God p
   that we should walk in them" (Ephesians 2:8-10)
   of this verse that states what does *not* save us.

Think about these things until you fully understan
God to give you someone with whom you might share
this week. There is such joy in proclaiming God's go;
about leading the person to Him; that is God's job. S
reap. God gives the increase (John 4:37; 1 Corinthians 3

c. Acts 26:15-20 (Note: These verses are right in the middle of Paul's testimony before Agrippa, so you might want to read the entire testimony.)

Repentance causes a person to see that Jesus is God and that He is to be honored as God. As children of God, we will be expected to honor God as God rather than being our own gods! To acknowledge His rightful place as God is to be willing to be saved from sin. When Adam and Eve chose to disobey God in the garden of Eden, they chose to be like God, to be their own god.

Salvation reverses this choice. A person coming to salvation is no longer a law unto himself but is willing to submit to God and to God's holy commandments. Why? Because salvation does not make us lawless; it makes us righteous.

3. People can't change their lives and become righteous. Only God can transform man, and He does it by grace through faith. If a person will believe on the Lord Jesus Christ, believing that He is who He says He is, God will do the rest. "For by grace you have been saved through faith; and that not of yourselves, it is the gift of God; not as a result of works, that no one should boast. For we are His workmanship, created in Christ Jesus for good works, which God prepared beforehand, that we should walk in them" (Ephesians 2:8-10). Underline the part of this verse that states what does *not* save us.

Think about these things until you fully understand them. Then, ask God to give you someone with whom you might share the gospel of grace this week. There is such joy in proclaiming God's gospel. Don't worry about leading the person to Him; that is God's job. Some sow...others reap. God gives the increase (John 4:37; 1 Corinthians 3:6-8).

— D A Y   S I X —

Let's continue to look at those things we need to know to understand the gospel of grace. There are many who fail to lay hold of the grace of God yet think they are safe in having eternal salvation. I believe people are in this state because they have not heard God's gospel but someone's version of it. The Holy Spirit convicts of sin, righteousness, and judgment, and *then* He converts. Therefore, as we've seen, we need to be certain to explain that a person is saved from sin, not just from hell.

When we deliver the gospel, we need to make sure people see the following truths in addition to the three we looked at yesterday:

1. Out of bottomless love, God took our sin and placed it upon Jesus. Jesus literally became sin for us. Thus, we can have forgiveness of sins and receive His righteousness. Look up 2 Corinthians 5:21, mark it in your Bible, and then write it out below.

Can you see what is exchanged in this verse? Doesn't it fill you with gratitude?

2. It is necessary to repent. Repent means to have a change of mind evidenced by a change of direction. Look up the following verses on repentance, and record the essence of what each verse is saying.
   a. Luke 13:2-5

   b. Luke 24:46-48

"Behold, I say to you, lift up your eyes, and look on the fields, that they are white for harvest. Already he who reaps is receiving wages, and is gathering fruit for life eternal; that he who sows and he who reaps may rejoice together" (John 4:35-36).

— D A Y   S E V E N —

I can't stress enough how vital it is that we allow people to see and understand the fact that they are sinners. Until then, they won't understand or appreciate the grace of God.

This is one of the benefits of reading biographies of the great saints of Christianity. These people had a real awareness of and understanding of their sin, and at the same time they saw their powerlessness to be free from it without God's grace. Many today don't see the awfulness of their sin, nor do they realize how it grieves the holy heart of God. Nor do they desire to be free of it. Instead they hope to get away with as much as they can.

Why? Personally I believe it's because we live in an amoral society. We have raised a generation of young people who have not heard the Word of God and who are ignorant of God's commandments.

How we need to keep the commandments of God before us in order to show us our sin! Listen to Paul's story in Romans 7:7-10, and then answer the questions which follow.

What shall we say then? Is the Law sin? May it never be! On the contrary, I would not have come to know sin except through the Law; for I would not have known about coveting if the Law had not said, "YOU SHALL NOT COVET." But sin, taking opportunity through the commandment, produced in me coveting of every kind; for apart from the Law sin is dead. And I was once alive apart from the Law; but when the commandment came, sin became alive, and I died; and this commandment, which was to result in life, proved to result in death for me.

1. What commandment does Paul use as an illustration?

2. How did Paul happen to know that he was doing this?

3. When Paul says that "apart from the Law sin is dead," he is not saying that sin was not present in him—did not exist in him—but that it was "dormant." It was there but not recognizable. When the commandment came, what happened to sin?

4. How did the commandment result in death for Paul?

You know, I think we forget that Jesus came into the world to save sinners. I think we overlook the fact that there won't be any salvation for us until we acknowledge our sin. "It is a trustworthy statement, deserving full acceptance, that Christ Jesus came into the world to save sinners, among whom I am foremost of all" (1 Timothy 1:15).

In Romans 7 we see that the Law exposed or brought to life what was already there—sin! Dormant, asleep, seemingly nonexistent but there and raising its ugly head when it heard "Thou shall not...."

Beloved, use the holy Law of God to help men see their sin. Allow conviction to settle in. Don't seek to bypass this crucial work of God. Don't be premature in seeking to relieve people of their misery. Wait and pray. God is "not wishing for any to perish but for all to come to repentance" (2 Peter 3:9).

Just this past week I received an exciting letter from a young woman we have ministered to through the mail. She sums up what I have been sharing these past two weeks about sin, repentance, and salvation. Listen to what she wrote:

> After studying the Scriptures and your devotional booklet you sent me, I learned what sin actually is. In the Garden of Eden sin was man wanting to be like God. Sin is man saying, "I don't need you, God. I can be my own God." Sin is independence from God. It wasn't until I defined sin that I was able to see and understand why Jesus must be God, Lord, Master, and Ruler in my life and heart. Before, I had asked Jesus to be my personal Savior, but I never surrendered my will and desires and life to Him. I was still occupying the throne. I see now that that was not true repentance, and unless we repent, we cannot have salvation because sin is our saying that we will run the show without God. When we come to Jesus in repentance, we are saying that we can't do things our way, that He must have His way, and we are willing to allow Him to be in complete control.

"It is a trustworthy statement, deserving full acceptance, that Christ Jesus came into the world to save sinners" (1 Timothy 1:15).

MEMORY VERSE

He made Him who knew no sin to be sin on our behalf,
that we might become the righteousness of God in Him.

2 CORINTHIANS 5:21

SMALL-GROUP DISCUSSION QUESTIONS

In week two we learned that the Old Covenant was to serve as a school-master, or tutor, to bring us to Christ. The Law was to show us that we could not meet God's standard in and of ourselves.

We also learned that the New Covenant would make every provision we needed in order to live in a way that would please God. We saw that we could enter into this covenant through faith and faith alone, that we were not required to work our way into it.

We learned that upon our entry into the New Covenant, God would give us new hearts, that He would write His law upon our hearts, that He would put the fear of Him on our hearts so that we would not turn away, that He would put His Spirit in us to cause us to walk in His ways, that He would supply all that we needed—it was all of grace! We did not deserve anything because of our sin, but God in His graciousness made provision!

1. What did you see this week in Romans 3 about the Law?
2. How does this parallel what you learned last week in Galatians?
3. How does the Law set a standard for us and show us our need?
4. How does the Law expose our sin?
5. How does the Law serve as a schoolmaster, a tutor, in our lives, in the lives of our children, in the lives of our friends, etc.?
6. So often today, we hear a gospel that does not truly deal with the most important issue that lost people need to understand. What is the issue that we need to be certain they understand?
7. How is salvation often presented when someone shares the gospel? What do people often think of salvation as an escape from?
8. The lake of fire is the consequence of what?
9. What did God demonstrate in providing a way for us to be free from the bonds of sin?
10. If we cannot keep the Law, what hope do we have? How can we earn this freedom from sin?

11. What does Hebrews 2:9 say? How was Jesus able to taste death for you, for me?

12. Because Jesus paid the penalty of sin, what is man able to receive?

13. To receive salvation and forgiveness of sin, what must man do? Can one pray to receive Christ and continue to live the same way as before he prayed that prayer?

14. Did you receive the Holy Spirit by something that you did? How did you receive Him?

15. Our salvation then is salvation from sin. It is true that we are saved from the penalty of sin, which is the lake of fire, but what are we saved from in our daily lives as far as sin is concerned? Do we have to live in sin any longer?

16. If you are saved by grace, then what enables you to live daily over the power of sin in your life?

17. What did you see about the Law that will make you more effective in sharing the gospel with your family, with those with whom you come in contact?

18. When you share the gospel, what things do you need to be certain you communicate?

19. How can any person be set free from the penalty and power of sin forever?

20. How has your study of the Law this week affected you?

I WANT TO KNOW TRUTH IN MY HEART, NOT JUST IN MY HEAD

How my heart hurt when I read the letter.

I have only one question—how?

I am a glutton and a bulimic—how do I *not* eat?

My husband is a lazy drunk—how do I reverence him?

I long for a man to hold me both emotionally and physically—how do I stop the longing?

I have a husband but hardly any relationship with him—how do I not resent him?

I did a lousy job of raising the kids—how do I live with the guilt? Or get rid of it?

I was saved five years ago and have tried to live for God. How do I get "changed" instead of just "trying to do what's right" and failing miserably?

I know Jesus is the answer—but how?

I've come to the place of little hope, and today I feel like I've lost even that little bit.

If you can help me, I'll be grateful. If you can't, how can I not despair?

This woman says she is a Christian. Aren't Christians supposed to be able to live as more than conquerors? Yes, they are. And yet, my friend, do you realize that the despair of this woman is typical of believers today? Our problem is that we don't understand how to live in the power of His grace.

I want you to look up 2 Corinthians 4:7-12 today. But first I want you to note that in 2 Corinthians 3:5-9 Paul compares the two covenants. This understanding will help you see that the "treasure" mentioned in 4:7 is Jesus Christ. We have the treasure because we have entered into the New Covenant. The New Covenant is the ministry referred to in 4:1. Now with all that in mind, read the passage and answer the following questions.

1. Why are Christians constantly delivered over to death?

2. What types of "death" are referred to in this passage? What is the outcome of each? Record your insights on the following chart:

THE "DEATH"   THE OUTCOME

3. What do these insights tell you about the Christian's ability to handle adversity?

Why is it, then, that so many Christians live in defeat? I believe they don't understand the grace of God which not only brings them to salvation but which also enables them to live as more than conquerors! They don't know how to appropriate grace on a daily basis.

Before we go any further in our study, I want to make sure we explore the depths of the meaning of grace so we understand that grace is more than "unmerited favor."

Grace frees man from religion and brings him into a relationship with God. Grace brings life, but it is also the means by which we are to live and to please our Father God. Grace is key to our relationship with God.

The believer never comes to God on any basis other than grace. I cannot emphasize this truth enough! What peace, what life, what power, what confidence would be ours if we understood this truth and lived accordingly!

If you understand grace, you will never turn away from the blessing of God because you feel you don't deserve it.

Those who understand grace know we can never come to God on the basis of what we deserve. Nor do we come on the basis of what we have earned. Nor can we approach Him on the basis of something we have done that we think has merit. Those who understand the grace of God are ready to appropriate His grace on the basis of faith, and on the basis of faith alone—*faith in the God of grace!*

If you understood grace, you would never feel that you couldn't ask God for forgiveness or help because you had failed Him over and over and don't deserve to be forgiven or helped again. If you understand grace, you know that grace covers all of your inadequacies, all of your failure, all of your human frailties…and all of your sin.

However, a biblical understanding of grace will also cause you to live in such a way that you don't cheapen His grace by seeking to turn the grace of God into licentiousness.

It is heresy to think that you can sin that grace might abound! If you think that you can continue to live in sin because you are under grace, you insult the Spirit of grace (Hebrews 10:29).

Life lived according to the grace of God is not lawless! Rather, life under God's grace is evidenced by ever-increasing holiness.

O Beloved, from what you've read and studied, how well do you understand the grace of God? Where is the weak link in the chain of your understanding? Write it out. Seeing it in black and white will help you grasp where you are and what you need to believe.

– D A Y   T W O –

The grace of God is everything and anything that you and I will ever need made available to us in and through Christ Jesus our Lord. Grace is God's power at work. In order to really understand the grace of God, let's look at its *contrasts* and its *capacity.*

First, let's look at grace in contrast to debt. A debt is something one owes another. God is no man's debtor. It is man who has transgressed God's Law; it is man who is in debt to God. Man owes God a life of perfect righteousness. Yet, that is a debt no man can pay because "THERE IS NONE RIGHTEOUS, NOT EVEN ONE" (Romans 3:10). No matter how hard man tries to pay that debt, he can't. Therefore, God moves toward man in grace so that although "the wages of sin is death,…the free gift of God is eternal life"(Romans 6:23).

God's gift to man is eternal life through Jesus Christ. God is not man's debtor and, thus, obligated to offer such a gift. But "the grace of God has appeared, bringing salvation to all men, instructing us to deny ungodliness and worldly desires and to live sensibly, righteously and godly in the present age, looking for the blessed hope and the appearing of the glory of our great God and Savior, Christ Jesus; who gave Himself for us, that He might redeem us from every lawless deed and purify for Himself a people for His own possession, zealous for good deeds" (Titus 2:11-14).

If you read these last verses carefully, you will notice that it is all of God! Man is impotent to do anything to please or to help God.

I've been editing this chapter while flying to Florida. As I arranged my black briefcase under the seat in front of me and took out this manuscript, the rough-and-tough-looking man sitting next to me was playing the part of a gentleman, asking me what I wanted to drink. He was watching the progress of the flight attendants.

"Perrier would be great if they have it," I responded. Not wanting to appear rude, I looked up at him and smiled and then reached for my big black Bible to check a reference.

"You know," he said, "at first I thought you must be some sort of lawyer working on a case."

I looked at him and smiled again. "No, I'm a Bible teacher," I said as I tried to finish what I was writing.

"That's a pretty good thing to be involved in. Pretty necessary these days."

With that I thought, *I think my writing has come to an end,* as I asked him, "Are you interested in spiritual things?"

"Yes, isn't everybody?"

"I'm afraid not."

"Well, I'm interested," he replied as he looked me directly in the eyes. "The problem is I don't live like it."

With that, I was off and running, sharing my own testimony, weaving appropriate scriptures into it. How well I understood Eric Liddel's line in *Chariots of Fire,* "When I run, I feel His pleasure." My heart began to soar.

I had the opportunity to explain to Zack that he'd only be ready for salvation when he came to the place of total powerlessness—when he saw there was no way he could ever get himself fit for the kingdom of God or make himself acceptable to God. It was only when he was willing to say, "God, I can't help myself. I come to you just as I am. I want you to take my life over completely. You can do anything you please with me. I want Jesus' righteousness, and I thank You that He paid for all my sin so I can be righteous in Your eyes."

I asked Zack if he would read a book I had written. He wanted to buy it. I told him it wasn't for sale. There was only one thing I wanted: He had to promise he would read it and look up the answers to the questions in the Bible.

Zack not only agreed, he also promised me that he'd come to see us when he finished. He's rough—tough—has tried it all. Yet Jesus came to save people just like Zack.

As Zack and I talked about the Lord, he said that it gave him chills. The chills came when I told him how I had prayed when I sat down next to him. It was a divine appointment. I had no greater joy than to tell him so when I signed a copy of this book for him. I just "happened" to have thrown in one copy because there was a little extra space in my briefcase, and I thought, *I may need this book on this trip.* In the grace of God, I did.

Zack didn't feel as if God owed him anything. He simply knew he owed God a debt he didn't think he could pay. He knew he was totally incapable when it came to living a life that would please a holy God. He simply didn't understand grace. However, you can also miss the grace of God when you think God owes you something.

Therefore, let me ask you a question. Do you feel as if God owes you something? Do you feel that He is obligated to you in any way at all? If so, write it down below so that you can take a good look at it. Then, next to what you think God owes you, write out the reason you think He owes it to you.

GOD, YOU OWE ME   BECAUSE

Now, how does it look on paper? Do you think God owes you anything on the basis of who you are or what you have done? Romans 3:24 says that we are "justified freely by his grace through the redemption that is in Christ Jesus" (KJV). *Freely* means "without any cause within ourselves." Therefore, if we are justified—declared righteous when we were sinners—not for any cause within ourselves, grace is apart from debt. "Now to him that worketh is the reward not reckoned of grace, but of debt" (Romans 4:4, KJV).

Think about it, my friend.

— D A Y   T H R E E —

Have you ever had people tell you that they thought you were arrogant because you claimed to know without a shadow of a doubt that you were going to heaven when you died? I have.

They thought that when a person died, God, in all justice, weighed his good works against the bad, and if the good outweighed the bad, the person ended up in heaven! If that were true, salvation would not be of grace; salvation would be of works. As the means of entering into heaven, grace and works are incompatible. If salvation is of works, then it is not of faith. It is faith which unlocks the door to the grace of our Lord Jesus Christ.

Now then, let's look at the second contrast: grace versus works. Salvation has always been by grace through faith. Look up Ephesians 2:8-9 and write it out below. Then take a careful look at what it says. Note the relationship between grace and faith.

Grace and faith are inseparable. Romans 4:6 says, "God reckons right-eousness apart from works." How many people do you think really believe this?

I will never forget when I tried to witness to my father-in-law. I was a new Christian, and it was not long after the suicide of my first husband. When Tom hung himself, my father-in-law and mother-in-law wanted Tom's death announced on the front page of the newspaper without any reference to the way in which Tom had died. They wanted all of his achievements listed, and there were many of them. Tom was a top student. He was also an outstanding athlete, pursued at one time by Casey Stengel of the New York Yankees. Tom had pitched many no-hitters, and the Yankees and other ball clubs were quite interested in him. But Tom's dad wanted his son to make big money, and at that time baseball was not so lucrative! His parents were achievement-oriented. They had pulled themselves up by their proverbial bootstraps and had made it to the top financially. We talked about it quite often.

After I divorced Tom (I was an unbeliever at the time), I came to know Jesus Christ and was saved by His grace. I had not seen my in-laws since that time. Several months after I was saved, God brought me to the place where I told Him that I would remarry Tom. Soon after that a phone call came from my father-in-law, telling me that Tom had hung himself. I had never contacted Tom to tell him that I would come back to him, although I'd had the urge to write him. Now it was too late.

I know my father-in-law felt I was partially to blame for Tom's death…and I was. I had not been the wife I should have been to Tom. I had not taken his suicide threats seriously, nor had I properly dealt with them. I can imagine that my father-in-law wondered who I thought I was, telling him about the forgiveness of sins and eternal life which could be ours through faith in Jesus Christ.

It was a difficult time for all of us, and it is hard for me to remember exactly what I said to "Dad" when I rushed to Ohio for the funeral. I only remember that he became very loud and adamant with me as he told me not to worry about him. I do remember his response clearly because it showed me what he thought was involved in salvation. He told me, "I am just fine. You don't know how many bricks I bought for that church. Why, I practically built that church! I am a good man."

Nothing I shared convinced the dear man that his good works wouldn't get him to heaven. My father-in-law died several years later. For all I know, I will never see him again because he did not pursue God's righteousness "by faith, but as though it were by works." He "stumbled over the stumbling stone," the Lord Jesus Christ (Romans 9:32). Not because he did not know His name or what Jesus had done, but because he never understood his own inability to please God. Until you see that, you can't see your need of grace.

He did not understand that if salvation is by works, it cannot be of grace. Grace can't be earned or deserved, and it is by grace that we are saved through faith (Ephesians 2:8). Grace is seen in contrast to works.

O my friend, I want you to read these verses in their context to know what "side of the page" they're on in your Bible. I want you to underline them or highlight them so they jump off the page.

1. Look up Romans 10:3 and write out below why these people missed grace and the righteousness of God.

2. Now look up Romans 4:5.
   a. According to this verse, who is justified and how?

   b. Would this affect you? Why?

We have much to be thankful for as children of God, don't we?

— D A Y   F O U R —

Salvation has always been by grace—even in Old Testament times. However, by the time of Jesus' birth, the scribes and Pharisees had eroded that truth.

The Jews sought a righteousness through the Law. They codified the Law, adding to it 613 statutes: 365 negative statutes and 248 positive ones. They felt that by adhering to these they would have kept the Law. Thus, they believed God would be obligated to grant them entrance into His kingdom.

When Jesus stepped into public ministry, the Jewish leaders were blind to their need of atonement for their sins. They were looking for Messiah, the King who would give Israel authority over Rome.

In Paul's epistle to the churches in Galatia, he confronts them with what he considers "a different gospel; which is really not another; only there are some who…want to distort the gospel of Christ" (Galatians 1:6-7). How were they distorting the gospel? They were teaching believers their salvation was secured by keeping the Law!

They did not see the contrast between grace and law. This brings us to the third thing grace is in contrast to!

1. Look up Galatians 2:16. Highlight it in your Bible and then record what this verse says about grace and the Law.

2. Second Corinthians 3:5-16 is printed out for you. Read it carefully and watch for the contrasts between the covenants of grace and law.

◗ 2 CORINTHIANS 3:5-16

5 Not that we are adequate in ourselves to consider anything as coming from ourselves, but our adequacy is from God,

6 who also made us adequate as servants of a new covenant, not of the letter, but of the Spirit; for the letter kills, but the Spirit gives life.

7 But if the ministry of death, in letters engraved on stones, came with glory, so that the sons of Israel could not look intently at the face of Moses because of the glory of his face, fading as it was,

8 how shall the ministry of the Spirit fail to be even more with glory?

9 For if the ministry of condemnation has glory, much more does the ministry of righteousness abound in glory.

10 For indeed what had glory, in this case has no glory on account of the glory that surpasses it.

11 For if that which fades away was with glory, much more that which remains is in glory.

12 Having therefore such a hope, we use great boldness in our speech,

13 and are not as Moses, who used to put a veil over his face that the sons of Israel might not look intently at the end of what was fading away.

14 But their minds were hardened; for until this very day at the reading of the old covenant the same veil remains unlifted, because it is removed in Christ.

15 But to this day whenever Moses is read, a veil lies over their heart;

16 but whenever a man turns to the Lord, the veil is taken away.

a. List everything you learn from this passage about the two covenants:

THE OLD COVENANT: LAW   THE NEW COVENANT: GRACE

b. Why did Moses put a veil over his face? What was going to fade away or eventually be replaced?

c. What happens to the veil when a person comes to know Jesus Christ? Why?

My friend, has the veil been lifted from your eyes? Have you really seen that there is no way you can be saved apart from grace? Have you seen—really seen—that you can't live each day in a way that pleases, except by His grace?

3. Read Galatians 5:2-4. Remember circumcision was the sign of the Old Covenant. Circumcision was to the Old Covenant what baptism is to the New.
   a. If a person sought circumcision, why was Christ of no benefit?

   b. If a person tries to be righteous in God's eyes (justified) by keeping the Law, what is his relationship to grace?

Have you seen the black-and-white difference between grace and the Law? Do you understand what Paul meant when he said that if you are "seeking to be justified by law; you have fallen from grace" (Galatians 5:4)? Paul was not saying you can lose your salvation and, thus, fall from grace. Rather, he was making a point of the fact that law and grace are incompatible. You are justified by one or the other, not both. And if it is by law, then you are obligated to keep the whole Law (Galatians 5:3). Otherwise, there is no justification.

O Beloved, there is only one man who has ever kept the whole Law: Jesus Christ. Why then, having begun the Christian life by the Spirit, do we think we can be perfected by the flesh (Galatians 3:3)?

"If righteousness comes through the Law, then Christ died needlessly" (Galatians 2:21).

Think on it.

— D A Y   F I V E —

Although I don't personally meet most of my radio listeners, many consider me their friend, a friend they can pour their hearts out to. They seem to know I'll sift carefully, listening to their problems and telling them if they are wrong. They trust I'll never reject them.

Not long ago I received a letter from a woman who had been raised by godly parents. At the sensitive age of four, her heart was terrified of the thoughts of a fiery hell. She did the one thing that she was told could deliver her from this eternal torment—she asked Jesus to come into her heart.

In high school she did everything short of physically losing her virginity. However, she was never really troubled in her conscience because she had always heard that if "we confess our sins, He is faithful and just to forgive us our sins." She was also taught never to doubt God. She wrote: "If we ask Him to come into our hearts (a phrase which now I highly disregard and discourage my children from using), He does, and it is a sin to doubt Him." Although she was immoral, she thought she was a carnal Christian. Although she was concerned, she wasn't concerned enough to change her ways.

Marriage did not stop her promiscuity. In one year she got involved with three men. When she got caught in one of the affairs, a "friend walked me through the plan of salvation and I made another profession and even got baptized. Now when I look back on that profession, it is one of the worst sins I have committed—to use God as a reason to hide behind my sin. I have wept more over that than just about anything. Now I see that when I made that profession of faith, I did it so they would think I was immoral because I wasn't saved."

Several years later she once again became involved with men. She went from bad to worse. She had sunk into a pit dug with her own hands. When she finally decided that she wanted out, she found it impossible. She couldn't free herself from her sin.

Now for the first time in her life, she has seen herself as a sinner—guilty, condemned, and without hope. And she wonders if she can live this way much longer.

> It seems like it would be presumption upon God's grace if He were to forgive someone like me. I mean, I have been so close to the truth all my life, but I have never known it for myself. I have even claimed to know Christ, but in reality, it's been just a false profession. Does the Bible say anywhere that God will save one like me? Never ever have I understood the doctrines of salvation, such as repentance and sanctification. Now, when I look back at my life, and as I read about the true conversions of other Christians, I can see that mine was not real. Now what do I do? I am so afraid that it is too late or that I am one of those people that God will not save.

Maybe you've never sunk this low. But have you ever felt you couldn't come to God and ask for forgiveness again? You know you should have learned. You know you shouldn't have sinned again. You wonder how He could bear the sight of you, how He could bear to hear your confession again and again without finally saying, "That's it. That's all. I've had enough. How much do you expect from Me? Don't you know that you are asking too much?"

You are not alone. So many feel that same way because they attribute to God the limited capacity of man. They don't understand the capacity of grace.

Now that we've seen grace contrasted with debt, works, and the Law, let's look at its capacity to handle our sin, our failure, our inadequacy.

In Paul's epistle to the Romans we see the clearest explanation, in all of Scripture, of the capacity of grace. Let's look at Romans 5:12-21.

▶ ROMANS 5:12-21

12 Therefore, just as through one man sin entered into the world, and death through sin, and so death spread to all men, because all sinned—

13 for until the Law sin was in the world; but sin is not imputed when there is no law.

14 Nevertheless death reigned from Adam until Moses, even over those who had not sinned in the likeness of the offense of Adam, who is a type of Him who was to come.

15 But the free gift is not like the transgression. For if by the transgression of the one the many died, much more did the grace of God and the gift by the grace of the one Man, Jesus Christ, abound to the many.

16 And the gift is not like that which came through the one who sinned; for on the one hand the judgment arose from one transgression resulting in condemnation, but on the other hand the free gift arose from many trans-gressions resulting in justification.

17 For if by the transgression of the one, death reigned through the one,

much more those who receive the abundance of grace and of the gift of right-eousness will reign in life through the One, Jesus Christ.

18 So then as through one transgression there resulted condemnation to all men, even so through one act of righteousness there resulted justification of life to all men.

19 For as through the one man's disobedience the many were made sin-ners, even so through the obedience of the One the many will be made righteous.

20 And the Law came in that the transgression might increase; but where sin increased, grace abounded all the more,

21 that, as sin reigned in death, even so grace might reign through right-eousness to eternal life through Jesus Christ our Lord.

1. Read through the text again, and mark every reference to Adam (including pronouns) with a stick figure like this: Adam. Also mark "one man," which refers to Adam.

2. Mark each reference to our Lord Jesus Christ with a cross. Be sure to mark the pronouns and every "One" which refers to Him.

3. Read through the text one more time, and mark the following words:
   a. sin, transgression (Mark these two in the same way.)
   b. death
   c. grace
   d. gift
   e. righteousness

4. Finally, list under the appropriate column the points you learn about what happened through Adam and through Jesus Christ.

ADAM   THE LORD JESUS CHRIST

— *D A Y   S I X* —

All of mankind falls under one of two federal heads: the first Adam or the last Adam.

Read 1 Corinthians 15:45-48 carefully and list in the appropriate column what you learn from the text about the two "Adams."

So also it is written, "The first MAN, Adam, BECAME A LIVING SOUL." The last Adam became a life-giving spirit. However, the spiritual is not first, but the natural; then the spiritual. The first man is from the earth, earthy; the second man is from heaven. As is the earthy, so also are those who are earthy; and as is the heavenly, so also are those who are heavenly.

THE FIRST ADAM   THE LAST ADAM

We were all born in Adam. So we bear his image. Thus, as we have seen, we are born sinners. Adam's single act of disobedience made all his descendants sinners. As a result of his disobedience, mankind was condemned. Adam's sin and mankind's condemnation happened long before the Law was ever given. Yet, when the Law came, man's transgression increased. Why? Because now, even though man knew without a shadow of a doubt what God expected from him, he still did not obey. Thus, sin abounded.

But when sin abounded, grace did much more abound. God sent another Adam—not one born of the first Adam, but one born of God's seed, born of a virgin. This second, or last, Adam would also be tempted by the devil. Yet, He would not yield to temptation. He would not sin.

When Jesus, the last Adam, came, He brought the grace of God, grace which would cover not only Adam's sin but the sins of all mankind! Jesus' one act of righteousness would make justification available to all, restoring to mankind what man had lost in the first Adam.

What is grace's capacity? It covers the sins of all mankind from the time of Adam to the coming of the Son of Man. No matter how great our sins, how weak our flesh, how often we fail, grace abounds. It's impossible ever to do or fail to do anything that can't be covered by the grace of God.

But you may say, "Kay, you don't know what I have done! You don't know how weak I am. You don't know how often I have failed. How can God forgive me, accept me, restore me, use me?"

It is grace, Beloved! Not cheap grace, costly grace. Grace that cost the death of Jesus Christ, the innocent for the guilty. Grace that banishes con-demnation and brings justification. Grace that covers the inadequacies, the failures, and the sins of the justified for the remainder of their days. Grace that can do all that and whatever else you need because of its great capacity!

Do you live in defeat? Are you spiritually impotent because you are ignorant of the abounding grace of God? Stop, my friend. Don't let His grace be poured out on you in vain.

— D A Y   S E V E N —

Brownlow North was a ladies' man—handsome, rich, smooth on the dance floor, brilliant astride a horse. He found it easy to propose to nine-teen young women, one after another. All of them adoringly consented to this young man who swept them off their feet.

Raised by a godly mother who taught him the truths of Jesus Christ and earnestly prayed for him, Brownlow drank heavily and gambled con-stantly. When he reached thirty-three, it seemed his mother's prayers had finally been answered. After the near death of his son, Brownlow became conscious of his sins and went to Oxford, England, where he decided he would "read for holy orders."

He was set on becoming a clergyman in the Church of England. However, the Bishop became aware of Brownlow's past and denied him ordination. Disappointed, he returned not only to his gambling and drink-ing but began mocking anything that was righteous. He was not prepared to live righteously again.

At the age of forty-four, his body was racked with such violent pain that he was sure he was going to die.

Dropping his cigar he gasped to his son, "I am a dead man, take me upstairs." They helped him to his room, and he threw himself on his bed. "My first thought then was, 'Now, what will my forty-four years of following the devices of my own heart profit me? In a few minutes I shall be in hell.' At that moment I felt constrained to pray, but it was merely the prayer of a coward, a cry for mercy. I was not sorry for what I had done, but I was afraid of the punishment of my sin."

The housemaid hurried in to light the fire, while her master lay groaning on the bed. Unwittingly, she had a part to play in that night's work. "Though I did not believe it at that time," continues North's account, "that I had ten minutes to live, and knew that there was no possible hope for me but in the mercy of God, and that if I did not seek that mercy I could not expect to have it, yet such was the nature of my heart that it was a balance with me, a thing to turn this way or that, I could not tell how, whether I should wait till that woman left the room or whether I should fall on my knees and cry for mercy in her presence."

The girl struck a match, and the fire blazed up. At that moment she heard a movement behind her and turned round. To her astonishment her pagan master was on his knees—and praying aloud. "I believe it was a turning point with me," said North in after years. "I believe that if I had at that time resisted the Holy Ghost it would have been once too often."

The next day he told his guests that he had given his heart to Christ. "He seemed as if just risen from a long illness, and very gentle and subdued in manner." Family prayers were instituted forthwith, and his dissolute friends informed that "I am, I trust by the grace of God, a changed man." His aged mother, when he went to see her, said, "Brownlow, God is not only able to save you but to make you more conspicuous for good than ever you were for evil."

The past now caught up with him. Weary weeks and months of spiritual conflict assailed him. Temptations, doubts as to his salvation, the suspicion of those who might have helped but doubted his sincerity, cravings for the alcohol which he had abjured, all this put him through the fire. He read nothing but the Bible. His wife would hear him groaning aloud and find him rolling on the carpet, agonizing in prayer. He would listen greedily to the exposition of Scripture.[1]

One preacher said, "He looks as if he had been a servant of evil and yet he looks as if yielding wholly to God." Finally after six months of turmoil he began studying Romans and for the first time understood the grace of God. Brownlow was saved.

Months later Brownlow North, quite by accident, found himself filling pulpits in Scotland. He became Scotland's most popular lay preacher. People who had never attended church before flocked to hear him and were being saved.

One night, as North was about to enter the pulpit in a highland town, a man handed him a letter, asking him to read it before he preached. The letter reminded him in no uncertain terms of some of the more repulsive excesses of his past and ended, "How dare you pray and speak to the people this evening when you are such a vile sinner?" North mounted the pulpit and the service began. At sermon time he announced his text, looked down at the sea of expectant faces—and read out the letter. The hush was intense. He spoke again: "All that is here said is true. It is a correct picture of the degraded sinner I once was. And oh—how wonderful must the grace be that could raise me up from such a death in trespasses and sins and make me what I appear before you tonight, a vessel of mercy, one who knows that all his past sins have been cleansed away through the atoning blood of the Lamb of God. It is of His redeeming love that I now have to tell you...

"I'll tell you what I am," he would say, "I am a man who has been at the brink of the bottomless pit and has looked in, and as I see many of you going down to that pit I am here to 'hollo' you back, and warn you of your danger. I am here as the chief of sinners, saved by grace, to tell you that the grace which has saved me can surely save you."[2]

O Beloved, have you seen the great capacity of the grace of God? Have you drawn all that you need from its all-sufficient well with your bucket of faith?

What is keeping you from appropriating what God has so freely given you? Is there something about your life which you feel God's grace can't cover? Write it out below. Then consider it in the light of what you have already seen and in the light of what you will see in the days to come.

What my radio friend who was promiscuous needs to see with the eyes of faith is what we all need to see and understand: There is no pit too deep, no sin too great but that there is enough grace and *more* to rescue us and cover all our sins. Where sin did abound, grace did much more abound! That's what God said, and we must take Him at His Word. Have you?

Remember, "GOD...GIVES GRACE TO THE HUMBLE" (James 4:6).

MEMORY VERSE

For by grace you have been saved through faith; and that not of yourselves, it is the gift of God; not as a result of works, that no one should boast.

EPHESIANS 2:8-9

SMALL-GROUP DISCUSSION QUESTIONS

In week three we studied the effect of the Law in the life of an individual. We saw that the Law was given to serve as a schoolmaster, a tutor, to keep us until grace would come, setting us free from the penalty and power of sin.

We saw, too, that we never were able, never would be able, to keep the Law. And because God is gracious, He made provision for our sin through His Son.

We also discussed the fact that it is through faith that we come to salvation, that our salvation is totally apart from the Law. We saw how the Law sets a righteous standard, how it reveals our sin.

We also learned that grace saves us from sin, from the lake of fire which is the consequence of sin. We saw that people are not saved from hell, but from sin.

1. What will free us from our religiousness and legalism and thrust us into the freedom of a personal and intimate relationship with our heavenly Father?
2. What part does the Law play in our salvation?
3. Explain how it is possible to obtain salvation through your works.
4. What is the key that unlocks salvation? Do your works play any part in salvation?
5. Does living under the covenant of grace result in lawlessness for those who truly know Him and understand His grace?
6. What is the mark of those who live under the grace of God? What typifies their lifestyle?
7. We owe God a life lived in righteousness, but we are unable to give that to God because of our own sinful nature. What provision has God made for the person who desires to live in the way that God originally intended?
8. Is there any way we can pay the debt we owe to God? What must we do to receive the gift that God has offered to us?
9. How is it possible for us to earn God's favor?
10. Explain why Christ died.
11. If we are able to be justified by the Law, was there a reason for Christ to die?
12. How do you begin a relationship with your Father? What is your part in your salvation? Where did you receive the ability to do what was required of you?
13. How then can your relationship be maintained?
14. Upon what basis are we *always* to come to our heavenly Father?

15. At what price to our Father do you and I have access to the grace of God?

16. Explain the difference between the first Adam and the last Adam.

17. What is the limit of grace? Is there a boundary beyond which grace cannot extend?

18. Under which Adam do you live? Did you realize that there was a second Adam who had come to set you free from the slavery under which you were born in the first Adam?

19. As you studied this week, did you see that grace, grace, grace is the key to the Christian life? Have you in some way denied the grace of God in your life? What has been your response as you have studied this lesson?

20. How has this lesson affected you? Have you ever thought there was something in your past that was beyond the grace of God? What did you see this week that would allow you freedom from that?

21. When you see the great price paid for you to enjoy the freedom of grace, what is your response? What has changed in your heart this past week?

chapter 5

I Need Your Power to Overcome My Weakness

— D A Y   O N E —

S he was secure enough in the grace of God to die, but not to live. *How typical,* I thought, as I read the note handed me just before I left to grab a bite to eat. We were at the Gaither Praise Gathering in Indianapolis, along with ten thousand other people. I had just finished teaching a seminar, and I had another to do that afternoon.

It was a relief just to sit and munch on a hot dog loaded with onions. Although I knew I'd soon be back with the people, I thought, *What's a hot dog without onions. I'll use a lot of mouthwash.* Suddenly remembering the note I had slipped into my suit pocket, I wiped the mustard off my fingers and reached in to get it. The story gripped me.

In despair over a sin she thought she would never commit, this woman had taken an overdose several months earlier. God had graciously spared her life, but now she was ready to try again. The pills were in her purse. The letters to her husband and four children were written. Everything was set. When the Praise Gathering was over, she'd go home. Death was better than life. She wouldn't have to face anyone except God anymore, and surely He would understand. Life was too much to bear.

But at my seminar God had spoken to her. Hope had revived:

I am going to get rid of the pills, which will be a big step for me. I know I can't get any more lethal pills because of my prior attempt. Holding on to them has been a way out. Thank you for being open and sharing yourself and God. Please pray for emotional healing from memories that bind me to the past.

As I finished reading the note, I tried to learn who had handed it to me. No one knew. My heart sank. I closed my eyes, trying to remember. I had to get to this woman! My staff and I started to pray.

Peace came...and joy. I knew that if I needed to talk with her, God would bring her back. After all, during the seminar she had attended He had led me to say something that was not in my notes or in my mind. It surprised me to hear myself saying, "You may be sitting here listening to all this and be planning to go home and kill yourself. You may have your letters written and know exactly how you're going to do it and when."

The Lord has often done things like this during my years of teaching. Yet, it never ceases to thrill my heart or to cause me to stand in awe of our God and His sovereign ways.

It was the last day of the Praise Gathering. Where...how would I find her among that maze of faces? Would she have the boldness to come back to our booth and identify herself? Or would she linger around the table, expecting me to remember her and respond to her note? And if she came, and I didn't recognize her, would she again feel rejected? "O help, Lord!"

Help He did...because He's a God of grace. She and a friend came by the table, and her friend let me know she was there. In the midst of all that crowd, arms reaching across the table to get to the books and tapes, questions being asked, money being counted out, checks written, books autographed, and hugs given, at last I was asking her if she had gotten rid of the pills yet.

"Honey, you need to give them to me. I'll get rid of them."

"But they're my security blanket," she said, as she looked over her shoulder.

"Did you mean what you wrote me in your note? Are you really going to be obedient to God, to trust Him?"

"Just a minute…" and with that she was gone. Her friend followed her, stopped her, and then she was gone again.

"She'll be right back. She saw her husband and wants to wait until he's gone."

No sooner was the explanation given than she was back, pressing an Advil bottle into my hand. I slipped the bottle into the pocket next to her note, hugged her, and told her to write. She was gone as suddenly as she had appeared—but I had the pills.

At midnight, as we were packing up the books, a doctor who had attended one of my seminars came by to talk. Remembering the pills in my pocket, I took them out and showed them to him.

"Do you know what these are? Could they kill a person?"

He knew, and there were enough to kill more than one person.

I walked across the hall to the ladies room, pushed open the enameled blue door to the stall, opened the bottle, turned it upside down, and watched the little, dark beige pills hit the water and dissolve. I lifted my foot, pressed down on the handle, flushed the toilet, and knew that God's grace was sufficient to help her through all her tomorrows. After all, look at all He had already done! He was going to teach her that His grace was sufficient not only for death, but for life.

Oh my friend, have you learned that lesson yourself? So often we believe God will save us, but we forget that the same grace that saves us is the grace that keeps us, enabling us to survive day in and day out, no matter what.

Many have misconceptions about the Christian life. They feel that once a person puts faith in the Lord Jesus Christ, life should become trouble free. Yet, that is not what the Word of God says! I think these misconceptions exist because people don't know what the Bible says; they only know what they hear others teach. And what others teach is not always biblical.

1. Look up Philippians 1:27-30 and record what you learn about the Christian life from these verses.

2. Paul wrote Philippians when he was a prisoner of the Roman government. He had been incarcerated because of the gospel of Jesus Christ. In the book of Philippians he speaks of the conflict he endured. In an unprecedented way, in 2 Corinthians Paul spills his heart sharing many of the conflicts, trials, and pressures he endured. Look up the following passages and record the various types of pressures he experienced.
a. 2 Corinthians 1:8

b. 2 Corinthians 6:4-10

c. 2 Corinthians 7:5

d. 2 Corinthians 11:23-29

3. Now go back and put a star by any of the pressures you can relate to. You may be suffering abuse in one form or another and yet think that you can't put a star beside Paul's physical beatings because his came as a result of his ministry and yours didn't. But, Beloved, abuse is abuse no matter where or how it comes. So, if you relate *in any way* to any of the pressures Paul endured, note it.

− D A Y   T W O −

Today, let's take a closer look at the setting of 2 Corinthians 12:9-10 so you can grasp the flow of what Paul is saying. If you understand these verses, take them to heart, and live by them, they will make all the difference in your Christian walk.

As you read through the text, mark the following words and their synonyms: *boast, exalt, weaknesses,* and *grace.*

● 2 CORINTHIANS 11:16−12:10

16 Again I say, let no one think me foolish; but if you do, receive me even as foolish, that I also may boast a little.

17 That which I am speaking, I am not speaking as the Lord would, but as in foolishness, in this confidence of boasting.

18 Since many boast according to the flesh, I will boast also.

19 For you, being so wise, bear with the foolish gladly.

20 For you bear with anyone if he enslaves you, if he devours you, if he takes advantage of you, if he exalts himself, if he hits you in the face.

21 To my shame I must say that we have been weak by comparison. But

in whatever respect anyone else is bold (I speak in foolishness), I am just as bold myself.

22 Are they Hebrews? So am I. Are they Israelites? So am I. Are they descendants of Abraham? So am I.

23 Are they servants of Christ? (I speak as if insane) I more so; in far more labors, in far more imprisonments, beaten times without number, often in danger of death.

24 Five times I received from the Jews thirty-nine lashes.

25 Three times I was beaten with rods, once I was stoned, three times I was shipwrecked, a night and a day I have spent in the deep.

26 I have been on frequent journeys, in dangers from rivers, dangers from robbers, dangers from my countrymen, dangers from the Gentiles, dangers in the city, dangers in the wilderness, dangers on the sea, dangers among false brethren;

27 I have been in labor and hardship, through many sleepless nights, in hunger and thirst, often without food, in cold and exposure.

28 Apart from such external things, there is the daily pressure upon me of concern for all the churches.

29 Who is weak without my being weak? Who is led into sin without my intense concern?

30 If I have to boast, I will boast of what pertains to my weakness.

31 The God and Father of the Lord Jesus, He who is blessed forever, knows that I am not lying.

32 In Damascus the ethnarch under Aretas the king was guarding the city of the Damascenes in order to seize me,

33 and I was let down in a basket through a window in the wall, and so escaped his hands.

12:1 Boasting is necessary, though it is not profitable; but I will go on to visions and revelations of the Lord.

2 I know a man in Christ who fourteen years ago—whether in the body I do not know, or out of the body I do not know, God knows—such a man was caught up to the third heaven.

3 And I know how such a man—whether in the body or apart from the body I do not know, God knows—

4 was caught up into Paradise, and heard inexpressible words, which a man is not permitted to speak.

5 On behalf of such a man will I boast; but on my own behalf I will not boast, except in regard to my weaknesses.

6 For if I do wish to boast I shall not be foolish, for I shall be speaking the truth; but I refrain from this, so that no one may credit me with more than he sees in me or hears from me.

7 And because of the surpassing greatness of the revelations, for this reason,

to keep me from exalting myself, there was given me a thorn in the flesh, a messenger of Satan to buffet me—to keep me from exalting myself!

8 Concerning this I entreated the Lord three times that it might depart from me.

9 And He has said to me, "My grace is sufficient for you, for power is perfected in weakness." Most gladly, therefore, I will rather boast about my weaknesses, that the power of Christ may dwell in me.

10 Therefore I am well content with weaknesses, with insults, with distresses, with persecutions, with difficulties, for Christ's sake; for when I am weak, then I am strong.

Paul was under attack when he wrote these verses. A group of people in the Corinthian church didn't like Paul. They questioned his character, his apostleship, his doctrine, and they were rebelling against his authority. They also despised the way he talked and the way he looked.

At one time things got so out of hand that someone slapped Paul in the face (11:20). Thus, as Paul brings his epistle to a close, he does a little boasting in self-defense. In the midst of his God-ordained boasting, we learn more about the grace of God.

1. List everything you learn about Paul's boasting in this text.

2. What kind of an experience did Paul have that could have led him to exalt himself above others?

3. Can you imagine such a thing happening today? Can you learn anything from what Paul shared?

4. What kept Paul from exalting himself? How did he handle it? (Follow his progress step by step—what did he do first?, etc.).

5. Do you see any connection between grace and power? What and why?

6. When you look at your weaknesses, how do you feel and why?

7. If you were to apply the truth of these verses to your life so that you lived in accordance with their teaching, what would you do the next time you were made aware of your weaknesses, the next time you struggled, or the next time you suffered insults, distresses, persecutions, difficulties?

8. Why can you say that when you are weak, then you are strong?

9. Can you see any justification for a Christian committing suicide? Why?

10. Memorize 2 Corinthians 12:9-10. These verses need to be hidden in your heart so the Holy Spirit can bring them to your mind. If you will read them aloud three times daily (morning, noon, and evening)

for the next week, you will find yourself able to say them from memory with ease. Reading them aloud is the key.

It is my prayer that in the days and weeks ahead you will be overwhelmed by your understanding of the grace of God which has appeared to all men.

Grace and peace to you, Beloved.

— D A Y   T H R E E —

Yesterday we saw that God's grace is sufficient for the everyday situations of life. However, is it sufficient for our daily transgressions? What does a Christian do with sin?

After my first afternoon session at the Gaither Praise Gathering on "How to Live on the Edge Without Tumbling Over," I was approached by two women who were hurting. Both had been teachers of the Word of God, but they had sinned. They had failed to cling to the grace of God and had reaped the consequences. Their hearts were broken. Their question was "Can we ever be used again? Must we forever forfeit the joy of teaching again? And what do we do about our past if anyone brings it up to us?"

My heart went out to them. The pleasures of sin endure only for a season, and then comes the barrenness of winter. But there is also the white covering of forgiveness! Because of grace, spring can come.

They met me at the book table because one wanted me to meet her husband—the second one. Again the question came up: Could they ever really know the joy of serving Him again, or was that to be denied them for the rest of their lives?

Under the Law it would be. They would have been stoned. But not under grace. Grace covers. Grace grants new beginnings. I'm not saying that we can always serve Him in the same way or capacity. Certain leadership roles, such as being an elder, come at a high cost. However, sin repented of, confessed, and forsaken does not leave us in limbo as far as serving God.

As we talked, I handed them a copy of a previously published edition of this book and asked them to read the first day. John Newton was my God-given example of the sufficiency of grace, not only for sins past but for sins present and future. If these words distress you because you think they give people license to sin, bear with me. We will deal with that later on this week.

Let me tell you something about John Newton's life. His salvation was all of God's grace, yet he had another lesson to learn regarding grace. And so do we, my friend.

In a very painful way, he was to learn a lesson on grace that he would never forget. Grace not only delivers us from sin's penalty, but it is also by grace that we are saved through faith from the power of sin.

After John saw Polly and she gave her consent for him to pursue their relationship, he went back on another slave run to Africa.

John felt things were under control. He felt reasonably good about life. Romantically he was communicating with Polly, and spiritually he was in touch with God. Vocationally he was first mate on a slave ship and had been promised the opportunity of becoming a sea captain his next time out. What more could a young Christian ask? For a young man of twenty-three, who as yet had no compunctions against slavery, the future looked promising.

But the rosy outlook lasted only a few weeks. By the time the ship landed on Africa's west coast, as John puts it, "I was almost as bad as before." He had stopped reading his Bible, had become careless in prayer, and had no Christian fellowship. "The enemy prepared a train of temptations and I became his easy prey. For about a month, he lulled me asleep in a course of evil, of which a few months before, I could not have supposed myself any longer capable."

...In the hold of the ship were naked slave girls. It was customary for the officers to have their pick. Momentarily he pushed away the temptation, but then, "I was now fast bound in chains; I had little desire and no power to free myself." So he descended into the hold, picked out a girl, and raped her.

Off the boat he was provided "a black girl for his pleasure." His lifestyle reverted to his old patterns. "If I attempted to struggle, it was in vain."

Then illness struck. He was reminded of his previous illness in Sierra Leone and the depths into which he had sunk at that time. Would this be the pattern again?

At first he despaired of finding divine forgiveness; the "door of hope" seemed to be shut. Then in desperation, while very weak and almost delirious, "I made no more resolves, but cast myself upon the Lord to do with me as he should please." Forgiveness came; peace returned. "Though I have often grieved his Spirit and foolishly wandered from him since (when, alas, shall I be more wise?), his powerful grace has preserved me from such black declensions as this I have last recorded."[1]

John's lesson came in a hard way. There's grace to cover our sins, but there's also grace to keep us from sin. How much better off we will be if we learn to appropriate His grace every day when temptation gives its siren call. We must not neglect the means which God gives us for knowing and maintaining a life lived in the grace of God. "Are you so foolish? Having begun by the Spirit, are you now being perfected by the flesh?" (Galatians 3:3).

O Beloved, can you relate to this struggle? Write out your struggle below.

Remember, God's grace not only delivers from the *penalty of* sin, but it is also sufficient to deliver you from the *power of sin.* It is this last aspect of living in the power of grace that many of us forget.

Deliverance from the power of sin comes as you cease your striving in the flesh and cast yourself in dependence upon Him. When you are dependent upon Him, you will find His grace is always sufficient.

– D A Y   F O U R –

Failure can be overwhelming, especially if you desire to please God. You wonder how things can ever be the same between you and Him. How can you pick up the pieces and begin again?

Like my two friends at the Praise Gathering, you wonder, "Can God ever use me again?" "Does He even want me?" "Will things ever be the same again with us?"

Have you destroyed your opportunity for a meaningful and joyous life? Are you to live forever in the shack of your failure, barely surviving rather than experiencing joy, satisfaction, peace, fulfillment?

Do thoughts such as these visit you in your stillness and engage you in conversations of "what might have been if only"?

Are you frightened by the knowledge that God is in control? Do you wonder how He will deal with you?

Do you want to run but don't know where?

Or do you know that the person, the thing, the object, the situation to which you would run would only displease Him more?

Does despair offer to cover you in its worn blanket of hopelessness?

Do you want to hide from life's consequences, cowering in the corner of inertia?

Don't you know that you belong to the God of all grace?

Grace is God's heart laid bare. Grace is there to preserve you in the darkest night of your failures. Do not let His grace be in vain. His grace—sufficient for all sin, for all failure, for all your inadequacy, for all your powerlessness—is yours to claim.

Grace is the birthright of every child of God. Grace cannot leave you inert. It calls you to get up, to throw off your blanket of hopelessness, and to move on through life in faith. *And what grace calls you to, grace provides.* "The kingdom of heaven is reserved for those who become as little children, for those who look to their Father in loving confidence for every benefit, whether it be for the pardon so freely given, or for the strength that comes from Him who works in them both to will and to do."2

How often we fail to understand this truth! We fail to appropriate His grace which is there to cover our failure and to save us from despair. Instead, we seek to live in our own strength and to approach God on our own merit rather than on His grace.

Grace is unmerited favor bestowed on us at the moment of our salvation. "For by grace you have been saved through faith; and that not of yourselves, it is the gift of God" (Ephesians 2:8).

If it took grace to save us, how can we think that it takes our own skill to make it? Since our own efforts and merit couldn't take care of our sin and failure in the first place, what makes us think effort or merit can reinstate us in God's favor?

We will never cease to need our Father—His wisdom, direction, help, and support. We will never outgrow Him. We will always need His grace.

1. How are we to live when we've sinned? Look up 1 John 1:9 and Hebrews 10:22 and answer that question.

2. What about when we are burdened? Look up 1 Peter 5:7 for your answer.

3. What do we do when we're tempted? Read 2 Timothy 2:22. What does it say? And what example can you follow in Moses' life as seen in Hebrews 11:24-27?

4. In all these things, and in other daily situations, what does Hebrews 12:14-15 say you should do? And if you don't, what does verse 15 imply happens? What does that mean? Explain it.

It is my prayer that you will see the necessity of depending upon His grace, that you will learn to live day by day in the grace of God.

— D A Y   F I V E —

Christianity is the only religion in the world wherein man becomes totally dependent upon God and remains dependent upon Him for all of life.

To the Christian, independence is sin. It is the tap root of all our failures. Listen to this statement of James Orr in his explanation of grace.

> *Grace…*is an attitude on God's part that proceeds entirely from within Himself, and that is conditioned in no way by anything in the objects of His favor.[3]

The grace of God goes beyond the ordinary course of what we expect from a holy God. That's why it is hard for us to accept it in our daily living.

We simply don't expect God to deal with us on the basis of grace. Rather, we expect Him to react as we would react, to respond as we would respond. We forget that He is God and that we are man. We forget to think as He would think. We forget we must learn to live by His words and not by man's reasonings and philosophies.

Grace is one of the hardest truths for us to comprehend and to live by. It is my prayer—not only for you, my friend, but for me also—that our Father will meet with us in a supernatural way. I long for the grace of God to be so engraved on our minds and hearts that we will be freed from a lifetime of attitudes, misconceptions, and independence which keep us from appropriating His grace in *all* its sufficiency. Read Romans 12:1-2 and answer the questions that follow.

> I urge you therefore, brethren, by the mercies of God, to present your bodies a living and holy sacrifice, acceptable to God, which is your spiritual service of worship. And do not be conformed to this world, but be transformed by the renewing of your mind, that you may prove what the will of God is, that which is good and acceptable and perfect.

1. What is God asking you to do in these verses? Before you answer this question, let me simply say that the *therefore* is in the light of everything God has done for us through His gospel of grace.

2. According to these verses, why should we do this?

3. Why should your mind be renewed? How would you apply this to what you have learned personally about the grace of God?

Oh, my friend, the more you renew your mind, the more you will understand the grace of God which has appeared to all men.

– D A Y   S I X –

As your mind is renewed, you will think the way God thinks rather than according to man's reasonings. You will see your need for total dependence. You will see that the source of your problems is *not* a poor self-image or lack of self-esteem. Rather, as you see self as it is—*totally impotent and worthless apart from God*—you will realize the need to continually cast yourself on the grace of God. As you see your poverty of spirit, you will be released from thinking that your works could ever merit favor with God. You will finally see that all you receive from God is given—freely given—without any cause within yourself.

Kenneth Wuest, in his work *Treasures from the Greek New Testament*, writes the following about grace:

In the ethical terminology of the Greek schools *charis* implied ever a favor freely done, without claim or expectation of return.... Thus Aristotle, defining *charis,* "lays the whole stress on this very point, that it is conferred freely, with no expectation of return, and finding its only motive in the bounty and free-heartedness of the giver."[4]

It will help you tremendously, my friend, when you think of God's grace, if you remember these things:

Grace is given; grace is free.
God's grace is freely given without any cause within myself.
Grace is always given because that is the heart of God.
Grace is always given—never owed, never earned, never deserved.
Grace is a benefit bestowed, released by faith alone.

To bring home these truths, look up the following verses. Note what you learn about grace.

1. Romans 12:3

2. Romans 12:6

3. Romans 15:15

Thank God for His grace and ask Him to bring these truths to your renewed mind continually, especially when you start to think or act in a way contrary to them.

— D A Y   S E V E N —

As you learn about the grace of God, you must understand that grace is not license. I can't emphasize this enough.

Grace is freely given, available for those who are apart from Christ and for those who already belong to Him. It is appropriated one way and only one way—by faith. Nothing more, nothing less.

However, grace doesn't permit a person to live an immoral lifestyle. We have already seen that John Newton, as a new Christian, sinned grievously. Yet, there was grace to cover his sin. If he had failed to trust God's grace to cover his sin and failure, I doubt he would have written the hymn "Amazing Grace."

He wouldn't have been acclaimed as a hero of the faith. He would have remained a child of God, but a defeated one. Defeated Christians have little power and are not effective because they fail to appropriate God's grace. Grace is power.

Listen to the words of this powerful hymn, and you'll understand why it is still one of the favorites of Christians today.

> Amazing Grace! how sweet the sound—
> That saved a wretch like me!
> I once was lost but now am found,
> Was blind but now I see.
>
> 'Twas grace that taught my heart to fear,
> And grace my fears relieved;
> How precious did that grace appear
> The hour I first believed.
>
> The Lord has promised good to me,
> His word my hope secures;
> He will my shield and portion be
> As long as life endures.
>
> Through many dangers, toils, and snares,
> I have already come;

'Tis grace hath brought me safe thus far,
And grace will lead me home.

When we've been there ten thousand years,
Bright shining as the sun,
We've no less days to sing God's praise
Than when we'd first begun.

Although John Newton committed sin, sin was not his pattern of life. Remember that the covenant of grace gives the believer the indwelling Holy Spirit.

In Ezekiel 36:26-27, we read: "Moreover, I will give you a new heart and put a new spirit within you; and I will remove the heart of stone from your flesh and give you a heart of flesh. And I will put My Spirit within you and cause you to walk in My statutes, and you will be careful to observe My ordinances."

1. Who is speaking in these verses?

2. What is He going to do?

3. What will the Spirit cause you to do?

Read Romans 8:1-4 carefully:

There is therefore now no condemnation for those who are in Christ Jesus. For the law of the Spirit of life in Christ Jesus has set you free from the law of sin and of death. For what the Law could not do, weak as it was through the flesh, God did: sending His own Son in the likeness of sinful flesh and as an offering for sin, He condemned sin in the flesh, in order that the requirement of the Law might be fulfilled in us, who do not walk according to the flesh, but according to the Spirit.

1. List below what you learn from these verses about the work of the Spirit.

2. Why couldn't the Law do the same thing?

Jude was very concerned about those who were distorting grace. Listen to what he wrote in his brief epistle.

Beloved, while I was making every effort to write you about our common salvation, I felt the necessity to write to you appealing that you contend earnestly for the faith which was once for all delivered to the saints. For certain persons have crept in unnoticed, those who were long beforehand marked out for this condemnation, ungodly persons who turn the grace of our God into licentiousness and deny our only Master and Lord, Jesus Christ. (Jude 3-4)

Let me define three words used in this passage, and then I have one final assignment for you.

Licentiousness is moral anarchy...living as you please.

Lord is *kurios,* the Greek translation of *Jehovah* in the Old Testament.

Master is *despótēs,* one who has absolute ownership and uncontrolled power.

Now let's examine Jude 3-4 by asking the "5 Ws and an H" to see what we can learn.

1. To whom is Jude writing?

2. Why?

3. What were these ungodly people doing?

4. From what you have learned about grace and licentiousness, how would they turn grace into licentiousness?

5. When was this occurring?

6. Where?

Walk, Beloved, in the grace of God—but don't think you can live any way you please.

MEMORY VERSE

There is therefore now no condemnation for those who are in Christ Jesus. For the law of the Spirit of life in Christ Jesus has set you free from the law of sin and of death.

ROMANS 8:1-2

SMALL-GROUP DISCUSSION QUESTIONS

In week four we again talked about the fact that the only basis upon which the believer could approach God was the basis of grace. We looked at the great price that was paid by our heavenly Father in order for our sin to be covered and for us to have a way to come to Him.

We saw that this price was an act of grace and that we could do absolutely nothing to deserve the graciousness of God extended to us. It could not be bought by trying to pay our own debt. It could not be earned through works. It could not be achieved through the keeping of the Law. It was *grace*!

And as we marveled again at the grace of God, we began to see that it has no limits, that its capacity cannot be contained in human boundaries.

1. What is the key to being delivered from the power of sin?
2. Is it possible to live in total victory over your past, over your failures, over the pull of the flesh? How?
3. What hope do you have when you fail, when you sin?
4. Is there any relationship between grace and power? Share what your insights were as you studied and as you memorized 2 Corinthians 12:9-10.
5. Even though we live in the confines of a fleshly body that is weak against temptation and even though we are faced daily with the lure of the world and its enticements, what do we have available to us that will enable us to rise above the circumstances and be victorious? How is power perfected?
6. What are you and I to depend upon for even our smallest daily needs, for our daily direction, for all that pertains to our daily lives?
7. What is at the root of all of our failures in the Christian life?
8. Why is it so difficult for us to accept and rely upon the grace of God?
9. How do the truths you saw in Romans 12:1-2 fit in with our study this week on grace?

10. How does having a poor self-image and low self-esteem affect your relationship with God? Is there anything that self can do that is acceptable to God?

11. From what you have studied this week, how would you define licentiousness?

12. Does the grace of God grant us the freedom to live as we please?

13. What provision has God made so that we can live under grace and yet live in a way that is pleasing to Him? (Remember your study on the New Covenant.)

14. Is it possible to enter into the New Covenant and then to live any way that suits us?

15. When we do fail as Christians, is restoration possible? Why?

16. Does God ever react as we would react? God always acts from what basis?

17. Have you ever put human limitations on God? Have you thought that He would react in a certain way because that is how you would react? Have you released that misconception and stepped into the glorious liberty that is ours through grace?

18. Have you realized that there is some area in which you have taken liberty because you thought you understood the grace of God, and now you see that what you thought was liberty is really licentiousness? Have you dealt with that area and brought it under the grace of God and put it in its proper place?

19. How has this week changed your view of grace?

20. What things will change in your life as a result of this week's study?

6

AT TIMES I FEEL LIKE SUCH A FAILURE

— D A Y   O N E —

Have you ever been convicted of sin and felt like an absolute dog? I have. Sometimes I groan because I know so much of the Word, yet I don't always live in the light of everything I know. As I was writing this book, the Lord reminded me of a wrong attitude. I had to stop my writing and confess my sin.

Then, as I was going over the manuscript for *Lord, Heal My Hurts,* I was convicted again. As I read the last chapter, I came to the part on meekness. Meekness is accepting everything as coming from God without murmuring or disputing or retaliation. I had known that definition for years. I had taught it countless times. Yet, as I read what I had written, I was convicted. I had not been giving thanks in everything. When I made a mistake, I would moan and groan over my ineptitude, my wrong decision, or whatever! When something would go wrong, instead of bowing my knees in submission and getting up to go on in His grace, I would hassle over why I'd done what I did.

I had become sloppy in my spiritual "attire." If I fail to put on the attire of the new person I am in Christ Jesus and I fail to walk in meekness, it is wrong. However, to compound it with another sin is worse. I hate it when I sin, and that is the way it should be. But many times, because my flesh wants to "be perfect," I tend to stew over my lack of perfection and "what could have been if only" I had obeyed God in the first place. That should not be.

When this kind of mental stewing begins, your mind is like a plane diving headlong toward the ground, spinning round and round in your "if onlys." I'm sure that at one time or another you've seen a war movie where the pilot is in a daze, headed for the ground while the audience is on the edge of their seats saying, "Pull back! Pull the stick back!" Grace is the stick, the lever of life that keeps us on a steady course.

When I confess my sin, I need to go forward, believing what God says: He is faithful and just to forgive all my sins and to cleanse me from all unrighteousness (1 John 1:9). However, if I begin to hash over the consequences of my sin or to focus on "if only" or "why didn't I," I am ignoring the grace of God which is sufficient to override what I fail to discern or to distinguish, or what I do not get done.

Now let me bring all of this to an applicable conclusion so that you don't miss what you need to see.

What can you do when you fail to appropriate God's grace? When you fail to behave in a Christlike manner? When you fail to give thanks in everything?

You can defend or excuse yourself.

You can rationalize your behavior by saying you have been under too much pressure.

You can cover it. Just ignore it. Not face it. Deny it.

You can struggle, trying harder to be a better Christian.

You can blame others. (Isn't this easy to do—to say it is *their* fault? Or to say, "I responded that way because of him. If he hadn't done such and such, then I wouldn't have reacted as I did!")

Any of these responses is to fall short of the grace of God, because they do not deal with sin God's way. The message of the gospel of grace is that you can never, ever create a righteousness of your own that could ever please God.

Think about it. What do you usually do when you fail to behave as

God would have you behave? Pick out a fresh incident and write out how you handled your failure. Was that typical of you? What is typical?

— D A Y   T W O —

When you think of God, how do you see Him? It's important to have a proper perspective of God and your relationship to Him. Let me share a letter which so well illustrates this.

Dear Kay,

Thank you for writing me a personal letter. You're right. I do need to first look to my husband and his needs, and get my strength and direction from the Lord "so that he may be won without even a word from my mouth."

Kay, I know now that the Lord has been trying to teach me to put my trust completely in Him and Him alone. That, I see, has been a very hard thing to do, as the Bible was forced upon me all my life by my father, who was a Christian, but was very dictatorial.

I was raised in legalism and never understood the kindness or gentleness of a father. I now have a very hard time understanding that God is loving, kind, and accepting of me. I know that through Jesus, He accepts me positionally, but I always feel that I need to perform for Him so that I will keep His approval.

Kay, I couldn't trust a God like that. I see now that my view of God has been very warped. I was seeking the love and approval and constant attention from my husband that I really wanted from my father and from my heavenly Father.

In the past I have run from man to man, looking for the gentleness, the care, the compassion, and, mostly, the understanding that I have needed. When my own husband didn't always provide these things, I would run in my heart to another man. For an entire year, I've been wrestling with the fantasy "dream man" who would be there for me.

The Lord has been showing me that this is very sinful and that I need to acknowledge this as what it is—SIN. Kay, I have confessed this to the Lord. And now I want to change my ways. Even though I still deal with fear, I'm believing now that the Lord is my source and my strength.

In many ways I've looked at God as an Old Testament God full of fury, full of wrath, and almost unpleasable. The Law has dominated my life for so long. I just long to lie back in the arms of a Lord of grace and mercy and rest in Him. Isn't it odd that I've been running from the very One who will give me rest and assurance?

Lying back in the arms of grace!

Christians today need to learn how to deal with their sin once they have failed God. Many feel that God will turn away from them in anger, that the forgiveness which is theirs through grace will eventually dry up. Some feel that one day God will have had enough and walk away.

This kind of thinking is understandable if we measure God by man because this is the way we often respond to one another. We allow people to push us so far and then that's it. We walk away, no longer wanting to have anything to do with them. And because we have been treated this way, or because we have treated others like this, we think God will do the same. The cure for this misconception about God is a renewed mind whereby we measure God by what He says about Himself in His Word rather than by man's concept of Him.

As I said in the beginning of our study, when a Christian sins, he can run either to Mount Calvary or to Sinai. Remember, it was at Calvary that God inaugurated the covenant of grace as He put to death His Son, the covenant Lamb. Sinai was the mountain on which the Law was inaugurated as Moses "took the blood of the calves and the goats, with water and scarlet wool and hyssop, and sprinkled both the book itself and all the people, saying, 'THIS IS THE BLOOD OF THE COVENANT WHICH GOD COMMANDED YOU'" (Hebrews 9:19-20).

To run to Sinai is to try in some way to do penance for your sins, to do some sort of good deed to make up for failing God. If good deeds didn't work before, what makes you think they'll work now?

When you see your own inability, weakness, and insufficiency, and you struggle harder and harder to be better—to be the Christian you should be—you are running to Sinai.

Running to Sinai will not help. As a matter of fact, it will compound your problem because it will bring misery, not peace...frustration, not victory. Victory never comes through the Law.

Grace, Beloved; grace is what you need! Grace is found at Calvary.

And how do you run to Calvary and bathe in the cleansing power of the blood of the New Covenant?

First, agree with God. Call sin exactly what it is. Agree with God that what you did is wrong because He says it's wrong. Confess to God aloud. "If we say that we have no sin, we are deceiving ourselves, and the truth is not in us. If we confess our sins, He is faithful and righteous to forgive us our sins and to cleanse us from all unrighteousness" (1 John 1:8-9).

Don't struggle to be better. Don't determine that you are going to try harder. Acknowledge your need of His all-sufficient grace and go forward trusting in the grace of God. "As you therefore have received Christ Jesus the Lord, so walk in Him" (Colossians 2:6). You were saved by faith; therefore, you are to walk in faith. It may be one step at a time, but walk. You can say, "I can't," as long as in the next breath you say, "But, God, You can."

— D A Y   T H R E E —

Do you ever feel you just can't be holy? Do you think holiness is for the super saints?

Maybe you have even compiled a whole list of dos and don'ts, things you think spiritual people would and wouldn't do. You won't miss church, visitation, or Sunday school meetings. You work hard doing everything you're asked to do for Jesus and the church. You have tried to be super-spiritual, but you feel like quitting. You might be able to list a lot of accomplishments on your biographical sketch as a Christian, but you know it would be mostly just words. You know what goes on inside. You know what you struggle with. You know you fail behind closed doors.

The book of Galatians just might have the answer for you. Galatians was written because some people went into Galatia preaching a different gospel than the one they had heard from Paul. The message they proclaimed taught that a person might be saved by faith in Jesus Christ, but that he still had to be circumcised and live under the Law.

In essence, these false teachers were calling Christians to become proselytes of Judaism, saying that grace through faith was not sufficient if people wanted to maintain their justification. They were declaring that justification is obtained through the cross of Christ but that it is maintained through the Law. Because they did not denounce Christ or His work on Calvary, their teaching was not easy to detect as "a different gospel" (Galatians 1:6-9).

While we may not be hearing the same message, many of its seeds have drifted down through the centuries. And various mutations have blown into the garden of our thinking and taken root there. Consequently, we feel that somehow we can gain acceptance or favor with God by keeping a certain code of dos and don'ts or by doing good works. Such thoughts need to be uprooted because they choke out grace.

Read through the book of Galatians printed out for you. It is only six chapters long, and you will find it profitable for your soul, my friend. I suggest that you mark the following words in a distinctive way or color so you can spot their occurrence at a glance:

a. grace   d. law
b. gospel   e. promise
c. faith   f. Spirit

Tomorrow we will look at Mount Calvary and Mount Sinai. See if you can find the specific passage in Galatians that we are going to study.

▶ GALATIANS 1–6

CHAPTER 1

¹ Paul, an apostle (not sent from men, nor through the agency of man, but through Jesus Christ, and God the Father, who raised Him from the dead),

² and all the brethren who are with me, to the churches of Galatia:

³ Grace to you and peace from God our Father, and the Lord Jesus Christ,

⁴ who gave Himself for our sins, that He might deliver us out of this present evil age, according to the will of our God and Father,

⁵ to whom be the glory forevermore. Amen.

⁶ I am amazed that you are so quickly deserting Him who called you by the grace of Christ, for a different gospel;

⁷ which is really not another; only there are some who are disturbing you, and want to distort the gospel of Christ.

⁸ But even though we, or an angel from heaven, should preach to you a gospel contrary to that which we have preached to you, let him be accursed.

⁹ As we have said before, so I say again now, if any man is preaching to you a gospel contrary to that which you received, let him be accursed.

10 For am I now seeking the favor of men, or of God? Or am I striving to please men? If I were still trying to please men, I would not be a bond-servant of Christ.

11 For I would have you know, brethren, that the gospel which was preached by me is not according to man.

12 For I neither received it from man, nor was I taught it, but I received it through a revelation of Jesus Christ.

13 For you have heard of my former manner of life in Judaism, how I used to persecute the church of God beyond measure, and tried to destroy it;

14 and I was advancing in Judaism beyond many of my contemporaries among my countrymen, being more extremely zealous for my ancestral traditions.

15 But when He who had set me apart, even from my mother's womb, and called me through His grace, was pleased

16 to reveal His Son in me, that I might preach Him among the Gentiles, I did not immediately consult with flesh and blood,

17 nor did I go up to Jerusalem to those who were apostles before me; but I went away to Arabia, and returned once more to Damascus.

18 Then three years later I went up to Jerusalem to become acquainted with Cephas, and stayed with him fifteen days.

19 But I did not see any other of the apostles except James, the Lord's brother.

20 (Now in what I am writing to you, I assure you before God that I am not lying.)

21 Then I went into the regions of Syria and Cilicia.

22 And I was still unknown by sight to the churches of Judea which were in Christ;

23 but only, they kept hearing, "He who once persecuted us is now preaching the faith which he once tried to destroy."

24 And they were glorifying God because of me.

CHAPTER 2

1 Then after an interval of fourteen years I went up again to Jerusalem with Barnabas, taking Titus along also.

2 And it was because of a revelation that I went up; and I submitted to them the gospel which I preach among the Gentiles, but I did so in private to those who were of reputation, for fear that I might be running, or had run, in vain.

3 But not even Titus who was with me, though he was a Greek, was compelled to be circumcised.

4 But it was because of the false brethren who had sneaked in to spy out our liberty which we have in Christ Jesus, in order to bring us into bondage.

5 But we did not yield in subjection to them for even an hour, so that the truth of the gospel might remain with you.

6 But from those who were of high reputation (what they were makes no difference to me; God shows no partiality)—well, those who were of reputation contributed nothing to me.

7 But on the contrary, seeing that I had been entrusted with the gospel to the uncircumcised, just as Peter had been to the circumcised

8 (for He who effectually worked for Peter in his apostleship to the circumcised effectually worked for me also to the Gentiles),

9 and recognizing the grace that had been given to me, James and Cephas and John, who were reputed to be pillars, gave to me and Barnabas the right hand of fellowship, that we might go to the Gentiles, and they to the circumcised.

10 They only asked us to remember the poor—the very thing I also was eager to do.

11 But when Cephas came to Antioch, I opposed him to his face, because he stood condemned.

12 For prior to the coming of certain men from James, he used to eat with the Gentiles; but when they came, he began to withdraw and hold himself aloof, fearing the party of the circumcision.

13 And the rest of the Jews joined him in hypocrisy, with the result that even Barnabas was carried away by their hypocrisy.

14 But when I saw that they were not straightforward about the truth of the gospel, I said to Cephas in the presence of all, "If you, being a Jew, live

like the Gentiles and not like the Jews, how is it that you compel the Gentiles to live like Jews?

15 "We are Jews by nature, and not sinners from among the Gentiles;

16 nevertheless knowing that a man is not justified by the works of the Law but through faith in Christ Jesus, even we have believed in Christ Jesus, that we may be justified by faith in Christ, and not by the works of the Law; since by the works of the Law shall no flesh be justified.

17 "But if, while seeking to be justified in Christ, we ourselves have also been found sinners, is Christ then a minister of sin? May it never be!

18 "For if I rebuild what I have once destroyed, I prove myself to be a transgressor.

19 "For through the Law I died to the Law, that I might live to God.

20 "I have been crucified with Christ; and it is no longer I who live, but Christ lives in me; and the life which I now live in the flesh I live by faith in the Son of God, who loved me, and delivered Himself up for me.

21 "I do not nullify the grace of God; for if righteousness comes through the Law, then Christ died needlessly."

CHAPTER 3

1 You foolish Galatians, who has bewitched you, before whose eyes Jesus Christ was publicly portrayed as crucified?

2 This is the only thing I want to find out from you: did you receive the Spirit by the works of the Law, or by hearing with faith?

3 Are you so foolish? Having begun by the Spirit, are you now being perfected by the flesh?

4 Did you suffer so many things in vain—if indeed it was in vain?

5 Does He then, who provides you with the Spirit and works miracles among you, do it by the works of the Law, or by hearing with faith?

6 Even so Abraham BELIEVED GOD, AND IT WAS RECKONED TO HIM AS RIGHTEOUSNESS.

7 Therefore, be sure that it is those who are of faith who are sons of Abraham.

8 And the Scripture, foreseeing that God would justify the Gentiles by faith, preached the gospel beforehand to Abraham, saying, "ALL THE NATIONS SHALL BE BLESSED IN YOU."

9 So then those who are of faith are blessed with Abraham, the believer.

10 For as many as are of the works of the Law are under a curse; for it is written, "CURSED IS EVERYONE WHO DOES NOT ABIDE BY ALL THINGS WRITTEN IN THE BOOK OF THE LAW, TO PERFORM THEM."

11 Now that no one is justified by the Law before God is evident; for, "THE RIGHTEOUS MAN SHALL LIVE BY FAITH."

12 However, the Law is not of faith; on the contrary, "HE WHO PRACTICES THEM SHALL LIVE BY THEM."

13 Christ redeemed us from the curse of the Law, having become a curse

for us—for it is written, "CURSED IS EVERYONE WHO HANGS ON A TREE"—

14 in order that in Christ Jesus the blessing of Abraham might come to the Gentiles, so that we might receive the promise of the Spirit through faith.

15 Brethren, I speak in terms of human relations: even though it is only a man's covenant, yet when it has been ratified, no one sets it aside or adds conditions to it.

16 Now the promises were spoken to Abraham and to his seed. He does not say, "And to seeds," as referring to many, but rather to one, "And to your seed," that is, Christ.

17 What I am saying is this: the Law, which came four hundred and thirty years later, does not invalidate a covenant previously ratified by God, so as to nullify the promise.

18 For if the inheritance is based on law, it is no longer based on a promise; but God has granted it to Abraham by means of a promise.

19 Why the Law then? It was added because of transgressions, having been ordained through angels by the agency of a mediator, until the seed should come to whom the promise had been made.

20 Now a mediator is not for one party only; whereas God is only one.

21 Is the Law then contrary to the promises of God? May it never be! For

if a law had been given which was able to impart life, then righteousness would indeed have been based on law.

22 But the Scripture has shut up all men under sin, that the promise by faith in Jesus Christ might be given to those who believe.

23 But before faith came, we were kept in custody under the law, being shut up to the faith which was later to be revealed.

24 Therefore the Law has become our tutor to lead us to Christ, that we may be justified by faith.

25 But now that faith has come, we are no longer under a tutor.

26 For you are all sons of God through faith in Christ Jesus.

27 For all of you who were baptized into Christ have clothed yourselves with Christ.

28 There is neither Jew nor Greek, there is neither slave nor free man, there is neither male nor female; for you are all one in Christ Jesus.

29 And if you belong to Christ, then you are Abraham's offspring, heirs according to promise.

CHAPTER 4

1 Now I say, as long as the heir is a child, he does not differ at all from a slave although he is owner of everything,

2 but he is under guardians and managers until the date set by the father.

3 So also we, while we were children, were held in bondage under the elemental things of the world.

4 But when the fulness of the time came, God sent forth His Son, born of a woman, born under the Law,

5 in order that He might redeem those who were under the Law, that we might receive the adoption as sons.

6 And because you are sons, God has sent forth the Spirit of His Son into our hearts, crying, "Abba! Father!"

7 Therefore you are no longer a slave, but a son; and if a son, then an heir through God.

8 However at that time, when you did not know God, you were slaves to those which by nature are no gods.

9 But now that you have come to know God, or rather to be known by God, how is it that you turn back again to the weak and worthless elemental things, to which you desire to be enslaved all over again?

10 You observe days and months and seasons and years.

11 I fear for you, that perhaps I have labored over you in vain.

12 I beg of you, brethren, become as I am, for I also have become as you are. You have done me no wrong;

13 but you know that it was because of a bodily illness that I preached the gospel to you the first time;

14 and that which was a trial to you in my bodily condition you did not despise or loathe, but you received me as an angel of God, as Christ Jesus Himself.

15 Where then is that sense of blessing you had? For I bear you witness, that if possible, you would have plucked out your eyes and given them to me.

16 Have I therefore become your enemy by telling you the truth?

17 They eagerly seek you, not commendably, but they wish to shut you out, in order that you may seek them.

18 But it is good always to be eagerly sought in a commendable manner, and not only when I am present with you.

19 My children, with whom I am again in labor until Christ is formed in you—

20 but I could wish to be present with you now and to change my tone, for I am perplexed about you.

21 Tell me, you who want to be under law, do you not listen to the law?

22 For it is written that Abraham had two sons, one by the bondwoman and one by the free woman.

23 But the son by the bondwoman was born according to the flesh, and the son by the free woman through the promise.

24 This is allegorically speaking: for these women are two covenants, one proceeding from Mount Sinai bearing children who are to be slaves; she is Hagar.

25 Now this Hagar is Mount Sinai in Arabia, and corresponds to the present Jerusalem, for she is in slavery with her children.

26 But the Jerusalem above is free; she is our mother.

27 For it is written,

"REJOICE, BARREN WOMAN WHO DOES NOT BEAR;

BREAK FORTH AND SHOUT, YOU WHO ARE NOT IN LABOR;

FOR MORE ARE THE CHILDREN OF THE DESOLATE

THAN OF THE ONE WHO HAS A HUSBAND."

28 And you brethren, like Isaac, are children of promise.

29 But as at that time he who was born according to the flesh persecuted him who was born according to the Spirit, so it is now also.

30 But what does the Scripture say?

"CAST OUT THE BONDWOMAN AND HER SON,

FOR THE SON OF THE BONDWOMAN SHALL NOT BE AN HEIR

WITH THE SON OF THE FREE WOMAN."

31 So then, brethren, we are not children of a bondwoman, but of the free woman.

CHAPTER 5

1 It was for freedom that Christ set us free; therefore keep standing firm and do not be subject again to a yoke of slavery.

2 Behold I, Paul, say to you that if you receive circumcision, Christ will be of no benefit to you.

3 And I testify again to every man who receives circumcision, that he is under obligation to keep the whole Law.

4 You have been severed from Christ, you who are seeking to be justified by law; you have fallen from grace.

5 For we through the Spirit, by faith, are waiting for the hope of righteousness.

6 For in Christ Jesus neither circumcision nor uncircumcision means anything, but faith working through love.

7 You were running well; who hindered you from obeying the truth?

8 This persuasion did not come from Him who calls you.

9 A little leaven leavens the whole lump of dough.

10 I have confidence in you in the Lord, that you will adopt no other view; but the one who is disturbing you shall bear his judgment, whoever he is.

11 But I, brethren, if I still preach circumcision, why am I still persecuted? Then the stumbling block of the cross has been abolished.

12 Would that those who are troubling you would even mutilate themselves.

13 For you were called to freedom, brethren; only do not turn your freedom into an opportunity for the flesh, but through love serve one another.

14 For the whole Law is fulfilled in one word, in the statement, "YOU SHALL LOVE YOUR NEIGHBOR AS YOURSELF."

15 But if you bite and devour one another, take care lest you be consumed by one another.

16 But I say, walk by the Spirit, and you will not carry out the desire of the flesh.

17 For the flesh sets its desire against the Spirit, and the Spirit against the flesh; for these are in opposition to one another, so that you may not do the things that you please.

18 But if you are led by the Spirit, you are not under the Law.

19 Now the deeds of the flesh are evident, which are: immorality, impurity, sensuality,

20 idolatry, sorcery, enmities, strife, jealousy, outbursts of anger, disputes, dissensions, factions,

21 envying, drunkenness, carousing, and things like these, of which I forewarn you just as I have forewarned you that those who practice such things shall not inherit the kingdom of God.

22 But the fruit of the Spirit is love, joy, peace, patience, kindness, goodness, faithfulness,

23 gentleness, self-control; against such things there is no law.

24 Now those who belong to Christ Jesus have crucified the flesh with its passions and desires.

25 If we live by the Spirit, let us also walk by the Spirit.

26 Let us not become boastful, challenging one another, envying one another.

CHAPTER 6

1 Brethren, even if a man is caught in any trespass, you who are spiritual, restore such a one in a spirit of gentleness; each one looking to yourself, lest you too be tempted.

2 Bear one another's burdens, and thus fulfill the law of Christ.

3 For if anyone thinks he is something when he is nothing, he deceives himself.

4 But let each one examine his own work, and then he will have reason for boasting in regard to himself alone, and not in regard to another.

5 For each one shall bear his own load.

6 And let the one who is taught the word share all good things with him who teaches.

7 Do not be deceived, God is not mocked; for whatever a man sows, this he will also reap.

8 For the one who sows to his own flesh shall from the flesh reap corruption, but the one who sows to the Spirit shall from the Spirit reap eternal life.

9 And let us not lose heart in doing good, for in due time we shall reap if we do not grow weary.

10 So then, while we have opportunity, let us do good to all men, and especially to those who are of the household of the faith.

11 See with what large letters I am writing to you with my own hand.

12 Those who desire to make a good showing in the flesh try to compel you to be circumcised, simply that they may not be persecuted for the cross of Christ.

13 For those who are circumcised do not even keep the Law themselves, but they desire to have you circumcised, that they may boast in your flesh.

14 But may it never be that I should boast, except in the cross of our Lord Jesus Christ, through which the world has been crucified to me, and I to the world.

15 For neither is circumcision anything, nor uncircumcision, but a new creation.

16 And those who will walk by this rule, peace and mercy be upon them, and upon the Israel of God.

17 From now on let no one cause trouble for me, for I bear on my body the brand-marks of Jesus.

18 The grace of our Lord Jesus Christ be with your spirit, brethren. Amen.

— D A Y   F O U R —

How did you do in Galatians yesterday? It's an interesting and much-needed book, especially in a society so caught up in humanism—the sufficiency of man.

Did you find the contrast between Mount Sinai and Mount Calvary? We will look at it in depth today.

Go back and carefully reread Galatians 4:21–5:1. Read this passage aloud several times. Also, in a distinctive way or color, mark each occurrence of the following words and phrases:

a. law

b. according to the flesh

c. according to the Spirit

d. free

e. slaves, slavery

f. bondwoman

g. covenants

Think on these verses, and we will discuss them tomorrow. Today, thank our God for the freedom He provided in Christ Jesus.

− D A Y   F I V E −

Do you remember how it came about that Abraham had two sons? Just so we won't miss the liberating truth Paul wants us to see in Galatians 4:21–5:1, let's do a quick review of Abraham's life. How well it demonstrates the grace of God!

Abraham was originally called Abram. He lived in Ur of the Chaldeans and was a worshiper of idols. When, by His grace, God called Abram, He promised that He would make of him a great nation (Genesis 12). So Abram had to have a child, but his wife, Sarai, was barren. Abram was seventy-five years old and Sarai was sixty-five. The promise of a "seed" to Abram and Sarai was not given just once. It was confirmed to Abram in a covenant agreement where God passed through the pieces of the covenant sacrifice in the form of a smoking oven and a flaming torch (Genesis 15).

When Abram was eighty-five or eighty-six, Sarai grew tired of waiting on God's promise. She was still barren. She was convinced that God was going to execute His promise another way; thus, she reasoned that if Abram were to have a child by her maid, Hagar, the child would be Sarai's child as well as Abram's.

So Sarai said to Abram, "Now behold, the LORD has prevented me from bearing children. Please go in to my maid; perhaps I shall obtain children through her." And Abram listened to the voice of Sarai.... And he went in to Hagar, and she conceived; and when she saw that she had conceived, her mistress was despised in her sight.... And Abram was eighty-six years old when Hagar bore Ishmael to him. (Genesis 16:2,4,16)

Now when Abram was ninety-nine years old, the LORD appeared to Abram and said to him,

> "I am God Almighty;
> Walk before Me, and be blameless.
> And I will establish My covenant between Me and you,
> And I will multiply you exceedingly."

And Abram fell on his face, and God talked with him, saying,

> "As for Me, behold, My covenant is with you,
> And you shall be the father of a multitude of nations.
> No longer shall your name be called Abram,
> But your name shall be Abraham;
> For I will make you the father of a multitude of nations."...

Then God said to Abraham, "As for Sarai your wife, you shall not call her name Sarai, but Sarah shall be her name. And I will bless her, and indeed I will give you a son by her. Then I will bless her, and she shall be a mother of nations; kings of peoples shall come from her." Then Abraham fell on his face and laughed, and said in his heart, "Will a child be born to a man one hundred years old? And will Sarah, who is ninety years old, bear a child?" And Abraham said to God, "Oh that Ishmael might live before Thee!" But God said, "No, but Sarah your wife shall bear you a son, and you shall call his name Isaac; and I will establish My covenant with him for an everlasting covenant for his descendants after him." (Genesis 17:1-5,15-19)

Now Abraham was one hundred years old when his son Isaac was born to him.... And the child grew and was weaned, and Abraham made a great feast on the day that Isaac was weaned. Now Sarah saw the son of Hagar the Egyptian, whom she had borne to Abraham, mocking. Therefore she said to Abraham, "Drive out this maid and her son, for the son of this maid shall not be an heir with my son Isaac." And the matter distressed Abraham greatly because of his son. But God said to Abraham, "Do not be distressed because of the lad and your maid; whatever Sarah tells you, listen to her, for through Isaac your descendants shall be named." (Genesis 21:5,8-12)

As you read these accounts in Genesis, aren't you awed with God and His Word? First God moves in His sovereignty in people's lives, and then later He uses the accounts of His workings allegorically to give us a precept by which we are to live continuously!

In the light of these scriptures from Genesis and from what you saw in Galatians 4:21-31, answer the following questions:

1. What are the two covenants to which Paul refers?

2. What covenant does Hagar represent? Where was this covenant inaugurated?

3. What covenant does Sarah, the free woman, represent? From which mount does this covenant issue?

4. Try to draw a stick-figure diagram of Galatians 4:21-31. It will help you remember it if you visualize it.

— *D A Y   S I X* —

When Paul wrote to those at Rome, he explained in great detail the gospel of grace. He wanted to make sure that they understood that justification would be by grace alone and not by works or by circumcision or by the Law. In Romans 4, Paul uses Abraham's faith in waiting for Isaac's birth as an example.

Let me jump right into this chapter and quote what Paul says. Then I will explain the passage and show you how it fits with Galatians 4. Watch for the words *grace, faith,* and *promise.* In fact, you may want to mark them.

▶ ROMANS 4:16-21

16 For this reason it is by faith, that it might be in accordance with grace, in order that the promise may be certain to all the descendants [Lit., *seed*], not only to those who are of the Law, but also to those who are of the faith of Abraham, who is the father of us all,

17 (as it is written, "A FATHER OF MANY NATIONS HAVE I MADE YOU") in the sight of Him whom he believed, even God, who gives life to the dead and calls into being that which does not exist.

18 In hope against hope he believed, in order that he might become a father of many nations, according to that which had been spoken, "SO SHALL YOUR DESCENDANTS BE."

19 And without becoming weak in faith he contemplated his own body, now as good as dead since he was about a hundred years old, and the deadness of Sarah's womb;

20 yet, with respect to the promise of God, he did not waver in unbelief, but grew strong in faith, giving glory to God,

21 and being fully assured that what He had promised, He was able also to perform.

What do you need to remember when you sin? You are under grace alone, not grace *and* law. Like Abraham, you are not to look at what you see or what you feel. Look at the promises of God. What God promises, He is able to perform. God promises you cleansing and forgiveness.

"There is therefore now no condemnation for those who are in Christ Jesus" (Romans 8:1). So, if you feel condemned, if you feel you must do something to make amends, to pay for your sin, to do penance, remember those are feelings. Feelings have nothing to do with faith. Faith is taking God at His Word, no matter how you feel or what you see or think. When God speaks clearly in His Word, you must not allow anything else to crowd out faith.

Cast out the bondwoman and her son! They represent the Law. Living under law and grace together is impossible. If it's law, it cannot be grace. If it's grace, it cannot be law. "It was for freedom that Christ set us free; therefore keep standing firm and do not be subject again to a yoke of slavery" (Galatians 5:1). You are a child of the free woman. Grace is her name! She became your mother through the promise, not through works or the Law or because God owed you a thing.

To be a child of the bondwoman is to be in slavery. That, Beloved, is what people are in when they try to come to God on any other basis than grace. People who can't accept that God will hear their confession and cleanse them from all unrighteousness chain themselves to impotence.

— D A Y   S E V E N —

Pride is thinking you can do something to assist God in dealing with your sin. Pride immediately shuts off the flow of grace. "GOD IS OPPOSED TO THE PROUD, BUT GIVES GRACE TO THE HUMBLE" (James 4:6).

Don't forget this scripture. Pride shuts the door to the grace of God because grace, as we have seen, is given to the poor in spirit. "No one is good except God alone" (Mark 10:18). It is grace alone which makes us "accepted in the beloved" (Ephesians 1:6, KJV).

The classic *Pilgrim's Progress* was written by a man who wrestled for years with grace. But once he saw the truth, the pilgrim made progress on his journey to the celestial city. John Bunyan's struggle to understand and accept the grace of God is familiar to many who, like him, see their sin but feel that they have to do something about it in order to be accepted by God.

Whether it is grace for salvation or grace to cover our sins as a Christian, it is only given to those who will humble themselves before God.

Submit therefore to God. Resist the devil and he will flee from you. Draw near to God and He will draw near to you. Cleanse your hands, you sinners; and purify your hearts, you double-minded. Be miserable and mourn and weep; let your laughter be turned into mourning, and your joy to gloom. Humble yourselves in the presence of the Lord, and He will exalt you. (James 4:7-10)

Do these verses seem contrary to your understanding of the grace of God? I can understand that. However, Scripture cannot contradict itself. James's words are a necessary caution we must keep before us whenever we study the grace of God. Here James shows us what our attitude should be toward our sin. We shouldn't sin and then laugh about it. Even though we are children of God and the penalty of sin has been paid, we must never treat sin lightly. The grace of God cost God His Son.

Grace is not license. Grace does not allow us to live in willful, continuous rebellion against God. Romans 6:14-15 states, "For sin shall not be master over you, for you are not under law, but under grace. What then? Shall we sin because we are not under law but under grace? May it never be!"

Grace delivers us from sin's reign. God wants us to remember that. Thus, in Hebrews 10:26-29 He puts a frightening warning before our eyes:

For if we go on sinning willfully after receiving the knowledge of the truth, there no longer remains a sacrifice for sins, but a certain terrifying expectation of judgment, and THE FURY OF A FIRE WHICH WILL CON-SUME THE ADVERSARIES. Anyone who has set aside the Law of Moses dies without mercy on the testimony of two or three witnesses. How much severer punishment do you think he will deserve who has trampled under foot the Son of God, and has regarded as unclean the blood of the covenant by which he was sanctified, and has insulted the Spirit of grace?

The person who says that Jesus' sacrifice is not adequate or who fla-grantly continues in willful sin, thinking, *So what? I am under grace,* is insulting the Spirit of grace. Anyone who thinks this way does not understand the grace of God or the salvation that it brings. He is blind to grace and open to the judgment of God.

The truths which I am sharing with you, my friend, are not easily understood; yet, they are essential if you want to mature in Christ. Think on them. Meditate on them. As you read God's Word daily, bring them before the plumb line of the *whole* counsel of His Word.

"And since we have a great priest over the house of God, let us draw near with a sincere heart in full assurance of faith, having our hearts sprinkled clean from an evil conscience and our bodies washed with pure water. Let us hold fast the confession of our hope without wavering, for He who promised is faithful" (Hebrews 10:21-23).

"Grace be with all those who love our Lord Jesus Christ with a love incorruptible" (Ephesians 6:24).

MEMORY VERSE

If we say that we have no sin, we are deceiving ourselves, and the truth is not in us. If we confess our sins, He is faithful and righteous to forgive us our sins and to cleanse us from all unrighteousness.

1 JOHN 1:8-9

SMALL-GROUP DISCUSSION QUESTIONS

In week five we learned that the key to deliverance from the power of sin is total dependence upon the grace of God in our lives.

We saw the relationship between grace and power, realizing that His grace is sufficient for every situation and that in our weakness His power is perfected.

We looked at the fact that the root of all failure in the Christian life is dependence upon self. We discussed how we must die to self and its ways and live in utter dependence upon grace in order to be what God wants us to be.

We learned that we need to be transformed by the renewing of our minds and that we are not to be conformed to the world so that we may prove the good and acceptable will of our Father.

Finally, we understood that it is by grace and grace alone that we should live our daily lives. God even made provision for us to be able to walk in His grace when He gave us a new heart and placed His Spirit within us when we entered the New Covenant. We also were reminded that grace is never license to do as we please.

1. When we run to Mount Calvary to have our sin cleansed by the power of the blood of the Lamb, what must we do with our sin?
2. What is God's response to this action described in your answer?
3. Once we have sinned, have run to Mount Calvary, have been restored to fellowship, what is the next thing we need to do? How must we look at our failure?
4. What promise did God make to Abram?
5. What was Sarai's response to waiting on God's perfect time to bring the promise to pass?
6. What was the result of her impatience, of her taking things into her own hands?
7. What was God's response to the situation that Sarai and Abram found themselves in? Was God faithful to His promise?
8. What conflict resulted because Sarai and Abram did not wait on God to perform His word?
9. How does the story of Abram and Sarai in Genesis parallel the study you did in Galatians?
10. In light of your study in grace, what is the bottom-line truth that you need to learn from the story of Isaac and Ishmael?
11. What can we learn from Abraham's faith? Did he look at the circumstances or at the promise of God?

12. When you sin, what do you need to look at?
13. Is it possible to live under grace and law at the same time? Under which covenant do you live?
14. Why did Christ die? Why did He set us free?
15. What causes us to be "accepted in the Beloved"?
16. What must our attitude be toward sin in order for God to be able to respond in grace? What is the attitude in us that God must resist?
17. If a person continues in willful sin, thinking that grace will cover, what has he or she not understood? What was the price of grace?
18. What did you learn this week that will help you not to look at the circumstances or at your feelings when these conflict with God's Word to you?
19. The next time you sin, how are you going to deal with that sin?
20. What did you learn about pride this week? About humility?

HOW DO I OVERCOME THE GUILT OF MY PAST?

— D A Y   O N E —

Tonight he would murder the queen. Slipping undetected into her bedroom, he went straight to his hiding place—the mammoth walnut wardrobe. Covered by a velvet gown, he rehearsed his plan once more. He would know when the queen had retired because her maid-in-waiting would bid her good-night upon leaving her room. He knew he could easily hear the door shut since it was a heavy door that shut with a bang.

There was a crack in the wardrobe door which kept him from suffocating among the thicknesses of her gowns. Through it he would be able to tell when the queen blew out the candle beside her bed.

He would wait for her breathing to change. Then he would slip out quietly in his stocking feet, walk to the bed, and rid England of her queen.

The rehearsing of his plan put him at ease. Loosening his grip on his dagger, he dropped his arm to his side. He leaned back against the strong boards of the ornately carved wardrobe to wait. It would be awhile before the queen even retired.

Suddenly the door of the armoire opened and a huge hand, fingers spread open wide, touched him. The groping hand immediately grabbed him by the shirt. In all of his planning the assassin had forgotten one thing—the queen's room was thoroughly searched each night before she went to bed. He was wrenched from seclusion.

The would-be murderer was brought before Queen Elizabeth. He dropped to his knees and began to plead with her to extend him her grace.

"Sir, if I extend unto you my grace, what do you promise for the future?"

With the keenness of a theologian, the man answered, "Your Majesty, your Majesty, a grace that propositions and a grace that bargains is no grace at all!"

The queen, seeing the truth of the man's bold response, said, "Sir, freely, by my grace, I forgive you."

Grace freely given won a convert. From that point on, the man was the most devoted servant the queen ever had.

This week we are going to look at the grace that serves, laboring in its King's service.

Look up 1 Corinthians 15:10, write it out, and memorize it.

— D A Y   T W O —

Grace is active.

And because it is, you and I are able to live productive lives which have eternal significance. Often we think of grace as merely doctrine that explains our salvation, something which occurred in the past. But grace is power in action. Oh, if we could only get this truth into our heads and then into our daily lives, what passion it would bring to our service to Him and for Him!

Remember, we saw that grace is all of God. Man just becomes the vessel to contain the grace of God. Consequently, when it comes to a life of obedience and service, even the desire and the power to obey and to serve God come from Him.

Our motivation to live for Him comes from Him. And our ability to do what He desires us to do comes from Him. *It is all of grace!* Listen to Philippians 2:12-13: "So then, my beloved, just as you have always obeyed, not as in my presence only, but now much more in my absence, work out your salvation with fear and trembling; for it is God who is at work in you, both to will and to work for His good pleasure."

Christians are the bottleneck! God doesn't tell us to work *for* our salvation; He tells us to work *out* our salvation. We are to carry out to completion that which God works in us. Philippians 2:12-13 assures us that God not only gives us the desire to do His good pleasure but that He gives us the ability to do it.

1. In light of that truth, you need to take a few minutes and search out where you are. Have you felt God urging you to a certain course of action? Have you felt there was something you should do, but you resisted either because you felt inadequate or because you simply didn't want to do it? What was it? Write it down.

2. Now go back and write why you can't or won't do it.

3. Tell God why you will or you won't carry out to completion what God wants to do in you.

You will see grace in action when you pull out the stops and let God be God in all of His power!

— D A Y   T H R E E —

There are four commands given to the child of God concerning his or her relationship with the Holy Spirit. Look them up and write them out. Note what we are commanded to do in our relationship with the Holy Spirit.

1. Ephesians 5:18

2. 1 Thessalonians 5:19

3. Ephesians 4:30

4. Galatians 5:16

The verb *be filled* in Ephesians 5:18 is a present passive imperative verb in the Greek. In the other three verses, the verbs *quench, grieve,* and *walk* are present active imperative in the Greek. The present tense denotes continuous or habitual action. The active voice indicates that the subject produces the action of the main verb. The passive voice means that the subject receives the action of the main verb. The imperative mood means that it is a command. In the light of these insights, look at these verses again. Next to each verse, record who does the action and who is responsible to see that it happens.

As you have probably seen, quenching the Holy Spirit keeps us from walking in the power of God's grace. Not to carry out to completion what God is working in you is to quench the Holy Spirit. To do that which is contrary to the character or commandments of God is to grieve the Holy Spirit. To be filled with the Holy Spirit is to allow Him to have full control. To walk by the Spirit is the same thing as being filled. However, in Galatians 5:16 we see that if we walk by the Spirit, we will not allow the flesh to fulfill its desires.

O Beloved, where do you stand with the Spirit of God? Is God's grace seen in your life?

— D A Y   F O U R —

One of the ways God's grace is seen in our lives—after salvation—is in our service for Him. To some, service may seem to be the opposite of grace.

Sometimes spiritual sayings become popular among different groups of Christians. Often these become good reminders of truths we need to focus on. But sometimes we carry these phrases to an extreme. Or we negate other truths with these sayings because we forget to consider the whole counsel of God.

For example, some say, "God is not interested in what you do. He's interested in what you are." Or "It's not doing, but being."

God *is* interested in who and what we are. He cares about what I am on the inside, and if I serve Him without becoming like Him, something is wrong. However, if we are what we ought to be, our lives *will* find expression in service for God.

Our service may not be something that others would necessarily see or recognize, but it will be there. Grace may call you to prayer. Grace may be expressed simply in your speech. Or it may be manifested through the gift of helps, mercy, or any of the other gifts listed in the Word of God. But it will be expressed in activity. Why? Grace is active and grace is power. Therefore, it will become active in and through you. Your responsibility is to carry out what God works in. He will be responsible for its impact. Wow! That's exciting!

Let's look at 1 Corinthians 15:9-10: "For I am the least of the apostles, who am not fit to be called an apostle, because I persecuted the church of God. But by the grace of God I am what I am, and His grace toward me did not prove vain; but I labored even more than all of them, yet not I, but the grace of God with me."

Suppose someone asked you how these verses show that grace is active. How would you answer?

As you read these verses, did you notice what I call "co-laboring in the work of God"? Paul says that he labors more than others. Yet, he goes on to say that it is not his laboring but the grace of God with him. See how beautifully what he says here fits with Philippians 2:12-13?

Paul understood grace! Here was a man who missed the earthly ministry of Christ, who was a persecutor and murderer of Christians, and who considered himself the chief of sinners and the least of the apostles. Yet he did not murmur, complain, fret, stew, or sit in a corner pouting. He knew that by the grace of God he was what he was. He knew that God had saved him in His time, not Paul's.

Paul understood that grace is active. What God bestowed upon him would not go to waste. It would not be in vain. He would serve God with all of the grace God had given him.

This, Beloved, is my prayer for you and for me.

— D A Y   F I V E —

Those who are genuinely saved and who serve the Lord fall into two categories: those who serve out of "knowledge" and duty and those who serve out of a biblical understanding of the awareness of the unfathomable love and grace of God. If you watch carefully, you can spot the difference.

The first will hold rigidly to the Law. They will be almost pharisaical in their Christianity, holding unwaveringly to standards, rules, or regulations, demanding much not only of themselves but of others. Many times they will struggle with God's unconditional love and acceptance. Their relationship with God will be performance oriented. In their estimation, whether God really loves them will depend upon whether or not they have "measured up."

Often they will keep people at arm's length, or they will attach themselves to another like a leech seeking love, security, approval, and a sense of worth. It's the only way they sense God's love for themselves. However, if the other pulls away or rejects them, they feel rejected by God. Serving God fulfills a need—theirs most of all.

What is the problem? Without trying to be all-inclusive in my answer, I would say they do not understand and accept the grace of God. And when one doesn't understand the grace of God, it is difficult to understand His unconditional love.

People who do not understand or accept God's grace are often performance oriented. In all probability, in the past they were accepted on the basis of their performance, either because of the way they did something or because of what they produced. From this acceptance they experienced a "pseudo" love. I say pseudo or false because it was a conditional love.

When they came to Christ, either their mind was not renewed or they had knowledge of truth but did not comprehend the depth of His love and grace. Whichever is true, it affected the way they served God. Because they want to please God, they serve Him, which is commendable. However, not understanding the grace and love of God, they serve Him in accordance with their "old" mind-set. And as I said before, they serve either under the legalism of the Law or in order to have their needs met. They serve to gain purpose or worth. They do not understand that it is only "by the grace of God I am what I am."

My friend, have you faced what you are—what you were—or have you covered it up? If you do not allow love to uncover it and grace to heal it, you will continue to serve God in the wrong way.

Think about it and write it down. What do you think makes you acceptable to God? What makes you unacceptable?

— D A Y   S I X —

"By the grace of God I am what I am." Do you really understand that statement?

Although you did not come to know God until a specific time, God knew you before the foundation of the world. Ephesians 1:4-5 says, "Just as He chose us in Him before the foundation of the world, that we should be holy and blameless before Him. In love He predestined us to adoption as sons through Jesus Christ to Himself."

What do these verses tell us? God knows you—all about you. Before the foundation of the world, He chose you. You may say, But surely God would not have chosen me because _____.

Because of what you have done? Because of what was done to you? Is that what you were going to say, my friend? Were you going to say that if God had known what you were—either by virtue of your own sin or by virtue of the sins others have committed against you—that He would not have chosen you?

You are wrong. God is *omniscient.* He knows everything. He's *omnipresent.* He was there when you did what you did. He was there when others did to you what they shouldn't have done. God is your *Creator* and the *Sustainer* of your life. He knew what sperm would meet what egg to create you. And He is the *Righteous Judge.* He judged the sin of all mankind at the cross when He put His Son to death as the sacrifice for the sins of all mankind.

However, for those who will not accept this sacrifice, risen from the dead, as their Lord and Savior, He will act as their personal Judge because they have refused to be reconciled to God. They have chosen instead to continue as His enemy.

As you noticed, there are five things about God which I emphasized in italic print. These five truths are taken from Psalm 139. This psalm is printed out for you. It contains truths that will liberate those who are held captive in the prison of their past. Therefore, I want you to take the time to go over this psalm carefully.

As you read, mark every reference to God, including *Thou, Thee, Thy, Thine.* Mark each of these alike in a distinctive way. (I mark *God* in my Bible with a triangle, as in the example.) When you finish, make a list in the space at the end of the about God concerning His relationship to you.

Psalm 139 is divided into four stanzas of six verses each. Over each stanza, note the best name for the aspect of God outlined in that stanza. The stanzas are broken for you by double spaces. Choose one aspect of God for each stanza from this list: Righteous Judge, Omnipresent, Creator, Sustainer, Omniscient.

❶ PSALM 139

[1] O LORD, Thou hast searched me and known me.

[2] Thou dost know when I sit down and when I rise up;

Thou dost understand my thought from afar.

[3] Thou dost scrutinize my path and my lying down,

And art intimately acquainted with all my ways.

[4] Even before there is a word on my tongue,

Behold, O LORD, Thou dost know it all.

[5] Thou hast enclosed me behind and before,

And laid Thy hand upon me.

[6] Such knowledge is too wonderful for me;

It is too high, I cannot attain to it.

[7] Where can I go from Thy Spirit?

Or where can I flee from Thy presence?

[8] If I ascend to heaven, Thou art there;

If I make my bed in Sheol, behold, Thou art there.

[9] If I take the wings of the dawn,

If I dwell in the remotest part of the sea,

10 Even there Thy hand will lead me,

And Thy right hand will lay hold of me.

11 If I say, "Surely the darkness will overwhelm me,

And the light around me will be night,"

12 Even the darkness is not dark to Thee,

And the night is as bright as the day.

Darkness and light are alike to Thee.

13 For Thou didst form my inward parts;

Thou didst weave me in my mother's womb.

14 I will give thanks to Thee, for I am fearfully and wonderfully made;

Wonderful are Thy works,

And my soul knows it very well.

15 My frame was not hidden from Thee,

When I was made in secret,

And skillfully wrought in the depths of the earth.

16 Thine eyes have seen my unformed substance;

And in Thy book they were all written,

The days that were ordained for me,

When as yet there was not one of them.

17 How precious also are Thy thoughts to me, O God!

How vast is the sum of them!

¹⁸ If I should count them, they would outnumber the sand.

When I awake, I am still with Thee.

¹⁹ O that Thou wouldst slay the wicked, O God;

Depart from me, therefore, men of bloodshed.

²⁰ For they speak against Thee wickedly,

And Thine enemies take Thy name in vain.

²¹ Do I not hate those who hate Thee, O LORD?

And do I not loathe those who rise up against Thee?

²² I hate them with the utmost hatred;

They have become my enemies.

²³ Search me, O God, and know my heart;

Try me and know my anxious thoughts;

²⁴ And see if there be any hurtful way in me,

And lead me in the everlasting way.

— DAY SEVEN —

The man who wanted to kill Queen Elizabeth did not succeed.

However, God did not stop Paul in his plot to put many to death. With a vengeance, Paul desired to rid the world of those of the Way who were polluting the Judaism he fiercely served.

Paul, who was then named Saul, watched Stephen collapse under the relentless pummeling of the stones. But he heard Stephen's last words:

"Lord, do not hold this sin against them!" (Acts 7:60). Although Stephen's bloody and noble death did not stop Paul from his great persecution of these "Christians," it did nag at his conscience. He continued to murder many, but it became increasingly hard to "kick against the goads" (Acts 26:14).

When the grace of God catapulted Paul to the ground as he set out for Damascus in pursuit of his enemies, the warrings of Paul's conscience came to an end. However, he still had to deal with reality. He had been a murderer, not of the wicked but of those who followed the Christ who now spoke to him.

> "Saul, Saul, why are you persecuting Me? It is hard for you to kick against the goads." And I said, "Who art Thou, Lord?" And the Lord said, "I am Jesus whom you are persecuting. But arise, and stand on your feet; for this purpose I have appeared to you, to appoint you a minister and a witness not only to the things which you have seen, but also to the things in which I will appear to you; delivering you from the Jewish people and from the Gentiles, to whom I am sending you, to open their eyes so that they may turn from darkness to light and from the dominion of Satan to God, in order that they may receive forgiveness of sins and an inheritance among those who have been sanctified by faith in Me." (Acts 26:14-18)

How did Paul deal with his sin? You know the answer, don't you? He dealt with it by understanding and accepting the grace of God. Paul never hid, buried, or denied his past. He dealt with it. That is why Paul could serve God the way he served Him and say, "By the grace of God I am what I am."

Was it because Paul understood, accepted, and lived in the light of the grace of God that he became the teacher of grace for the New Testament? I think possibly so.

I think this is why it's so easy for me to share my past. I understand the grace of God, so to let others know what I was is not a problem.

Rather it's a joy. Over and over again I've seen God use it to touch lives and give people hope.

When all I wanted was to excel as a wife and a mother, I failed in both. I had no other ambition as a woman. Being religious but not knowing God, I thought it was impossible to live with a manic-depressive. So I packed up my possessions, put our two sons in the car, and left. Lonely, longing for someone to love me unconditionally, and wanting to live without moral restraints, I shook my fist in the face of God and through clenched teeth said, "To hell with You, God; I'm going to find someone to love me."

As I have shared my testimony, some have been quite offended by what I said to God. I certainly can understand because it is offensive. However, I tell it anyway because it so demonstrates the love and grace of God. God did exactly what I said: He went to hell for me in the person of His Son because He loved me. And while I said, "To hell with You," He had already said, "To heaven with you, Kay." I just didn't know it at the time.

In my desperate search for love, I compromised every standard I once held. I not only became immoral, but I also had an affair with a married man. That was something I never dreamed I would do. And yet, isn't that the way with so many of us. We give in to sin and eventually find ourselves plunged deeper and deeper into its cesspool.

In all of this, I failed to achieve my second goal, and that was to be the best of mothers. My heart grieves if I allow my mind to dwell on what could have been had I known God or feared Him. The Law could have restrained me, if I had only heeded it, but I didn't.

All this time my husband was threatening suicide. Trying to bluff him out of it and not really believing that he was serious, I would say, "Go ahead and kill yourself so I can get your money." Bluff or not, to the hearer these words were like the noose he eventually put around his neck. As I shared earlier, soon after I came to know the Lord Jesus Christ, and before I got around to telling Tom I would go back to him, Tom hung himself.

It's not a very pretty past, is it? Yet, I talk about it. Not because I think everyone should do the same, but because I believe our Father would have me share it. However, it has caused me some problems—especially with those who are rigid and legalistic in their Christianity. If I had just been immoral, they would have forgiven me, but because I have been divorced, they won't. They feel I shouldn't be in public ministry. Yet, my divorce came before my salvation. They also forget (or don't know) that I was willing to remarry Tom, but he committed suicide. They ignore that my husband's death frees me from my marriage vows.

These people don't understand the grace of God—grace that is greater than all our sin, grace that takes us just as we are and declares us accepted in the Beloved.

What could happen if I chose not to share my past? What if those who heard me speak met someone from my past, someone who knew me before I knew Christ? I'll never forget what happened when they first introduced our Precept courses in Ohio. As they started the videotape and I came on the screen, one of the men in the audience suddenly leaned forward and said, "Wait a minute! I know that woman. That's Kay Lee. There's no way she could be saved." With that, he folded his arms, leaned back, and crossed his legs. His body language told everyone in the room he wasn't about to listen to me. You see, although I never knew him as a personal friend, he knew a lot about me.

When I heard about this incident, I sent him a tape of my testimony. I had hidden nothing about my past. I stood confident in the grace of God that abounded not only to Paul, the chief of sinners, but also to me.

I want to be open about what I was, and let people know what—by the grace of God—I have become. Then if people still have a problem with my past, it becomes their problem, not mine!

Let me take you to a passage which has meant so much to me. Maybe it will minister to you also. I know it will if you have a past you'd like to bury.

Read the passage, and then we'll take it apart to see what we can learn.

For the love of Christ controls us, having concluded this, that one died for all, therefore all died; and He died for all, that they who live should no longer live for themselves, but for Him who died and rose again on their behalf. Therefore from now on we recognize no man according to the flesh; even though we have known Christ according to the flesh, yet now we know Him thus no longer. Therefore if any man is in Christ, he is a new creature; the old things passed away; behold, new things have come. (2 Corinthians 5:14-17)

1. Who died for all?

2. What happened because of that death?

3. What do you think Paul means when he says that from now on we recognize no man according to the flesh?

4. How could you use this passage to minister to someone who has a past he is ashamed of?

I'll never forget when I discovered 2 Corinthians 5:17. I was twenty-nine and a brand-new Christian with an incredible hunger for the Word of God. I couldn't get enough. However, having two sons and a full-time job on a research team at Johns Hopkins Hospital in Baltimore, Maryland, kept me quite busy. So I decided to prop my Bible on my lap and brace it on the steering wheel so I could read while I drove to work every day. I know I must have really kept some angels busy! I was on my way to work when I read, "If any man is in Christ, he is a new creature, old things have passed away, all things have become new."

I thought, *God, I can't believe it! That verse describes me!* At the time I didn't know that this is true of every true child of God, but I was elated. I was brand-new!

Suppose you and I have the opportunity to meet someday. What will you think of me? Will you think *harlot, adulteress?* I hope not. If you do, you have the wrong Kay. The old Kay died. She was crucified with Christ and buried. The old man that lived in Kay was crucified with Christ, and Kay was raised in the likeness of Jesus' resurrection to walk in newness of life. Isn't that awesome?

Just remember, because of grace it doesn't matter what you were, it only matters where you are now…and that you are "in Him" and that "He is in you."

Now, let me bring all of this home to you. What do you know of the grace of God? Do you live in the light of His grace? Do you deal with others on the basis of God's grace? Or do you slip back into law because that is where you live?

I plead with you. Let love uncover your past, and let the balm of grace heal it. God, in His omniscience and sovereignty, allowed you to experience what you experienced. His intent was not to destroy you because His thoughts toward you are precious. Rather, His purpose was to use it all to mold and to make you into His child, a child upon whom He would delight to pour out His love. A child who would serve Him in the fullness of His grace.

In your life, what needs to be uncovered, dealt with, healed by His grace? Write it out.

MEMORY VERSE

Therefore if any man is in Christ, he is a new creature; the old things passed away; behold, new things have come.

2 CORINTHIANS 5:17

SMALL-GROUP DISCUSSION QUESTIONS

In week six we looked at the way in which we must deal with our sin by running to the foot of the Cross for cleansing and by agreeing with God about our sin. We saw that we must call our sin "sin" and be willing to turn from it.

We studied the story of Abraham and Sarah and the son of the free woman and the son of the bondwoman. God taught us a powerful lesson through what happened in this situation, showing us that we cannot live under two covenants — law and grace. We saw, too, that it was the bond-woman and her son who were cast out. Again we saw in picture form that it is all of *grace!*

1. Why are we not seeing Christians having a greater impact on the world for the kingdom of God if God truly is responsible to pour out His grace and enable them?
2. What keeps us from carrying out to its completion what God is working into our lives?
3. When we do not do what God commands or what the Word of God teaches, how does this affect the Holy Spirit?
4. How are we able to carry out to completion what God has enabled us to do? What gives us the power to be obedient?
5. Did Paul have any reason to think that he could never be used of God, that the grace of God could never cover him?

6. How did Paul overcome his past and come to the point that God could use him in the furtherance of the kingdom?

7. How was the grace of God manifested in Paul's life?

8. Was God surprised when Paul cried out to Him for salvation? Did God know who Paul was, or did God extend to Paul His grace and find out later that He had saved someone who had been persecuting His people?

9. Upon what basis did God save Paul?

10. Upon what basis did God save you?

11. Upon what basis are you serving God? Is it under legalism or to gain approval, or is it because of the love you have for a gracious God who has poured out His unfathomable love toward you?

12. Did you see this week that it is by the grace of God that you are what you are? Will His grace be poured out on you in vain, or will you serve out of love the One who paid such a great price to offer you grace?

13. What is the most basic truth you learned this week from your study in Psalm 139?

14. Was God surprised when you came to Him? Did He have any idea about the things you had done when you were walking your own way, doing your own thing? Did He know of the ungodly things that had been done to you? Did it affect His decision to accept you in the Beloved? Why?

15. What aspect of God's character is demonstrated by the fact that He knew all about you before you ever decided to come to Him? What does this mean to you now that you know Him?

16. When things seem out of control, when you have blown it, when you have been disobedient, when you have failed miserably, do you ever want to run and hide? Does it do any good at all to try to hide from God the things that we are ashamed of, the things that we don't want anyone else to know? Why? What did you learn about His character that lets you know that you cannot hide from Him?

17. How is the particular attribute of God alluded to in question 15 a comfort to you as His child?

18. Are you ever unhappy with the way you look, with your height, your weight, the length of your nose, the size of your feet, the color of your hair, etc.? Who made you? How do you know that He made you just the way He wanted you to be to bring Him the most glory?

19. Sometimes do you wonder how you will make it? Who is the One who will sustain you?

20. Has someone wronged you? Do you wonder how you will be vindicated? What did you see about your God this week that allows you to rest in Him regarding this concern?

chapter 8

I FEEL SO INADEQUATE

— D A Y   O N E —

I've sinned. And I know the Lord! Can I ever hope to be used of Him again?"

That was the woman's question at the end of a long letter telling me every detail that led her into an affair with her pastor. Her heart was breaking because she loved him, but she loved the Lord more. She couldn't endure the torment of her disobedience any longer. The pleasure of sin had come to an end. Now she wanted to know if she could ever again serve the Lord she had denied.

How I longed to tell this repentant one of the grace of God; yet, there was no way. Hers was another anonymous letter. Several days after I received the letter, I used it as an illustration in one of my teaching sessions. Little did I realize what widespread ramifications that would have.

A week later there was a letter in my ministry mailbox from one of my staff who had written the woman a letter, pouring out her heart. The staff member didn't know the letter had come anonymously.

It was just what this woman needed to hear, but how could I reach her? Once again I turned to radio. Maybe by telling her story on letter day and reading the letter from our staff member, I could find her and minister His truths over the air.

It worked…for not only did we hear from the woman, but we heard from many, many others—all of them wondering if they could ever hope to minister to others again.

This, Beloved, may be your question. Is there grace enough to enable you to minister to others...even when you have sinned? We will talk about that and even more this week. But before we do, let me share our staff member's response:

Years ago I, too, gave into thoughts which led to actions with a man in my church. We were both leaders. I was a Christian, vulnerable because I was not in the Word of God in the way I should have been. I thought I could handle it, but the Bible says we are to flee, not to "handle it." If only I had...

The situation lasted about a year. I was left devastated. I attempted suicide twice. Then God moved me to Chattanooga and put me in Precept Upon Precept. I was suffering—as you are—from all the memories, the longing for the person, the misery because I had failed God so badly, the fear that someone would find out. I was in agony even though I had repented and put it away six months before. I knew God had forgiven me. I knew He hadn't forsaken me, but I also knew our fellowship had been broken and it was not going to be the same for a while.

Then we had a conference, and I heard teaching on Hosea and Gomer. God showed me where I was: the adulteress (Gomer). He also showed me that my loving husband (Jesus) had gone and brought me back from the slavery of sin and shut me up in a room, not to fellowship with me intimately as we had before, but to allow me time to come to a point where He was all I wanted in the world.

Just knowing that was enough. I could be content to stay as long as He deemed necessary. My heart cried out that He was all I wanted. And He knew my heart. It wasn't two days before He opened the door to the room and let me out into full fellowship with Him. That was Valentine's Day, 1978. And it has been that way ever since.

If you will get into the Word in an in-depth way and allow time and the Word to heal you, you will survive. You will never get over breaking the Lord's heart so badly, but you will get to the place that you can grow and become mature and used of the Lord.

Today I am 100 percent whole. My relationship was twelve years ago. I am a gospel singer now and work at Precept Ministries. I can only stand in awe of God's faithfulness to me…and yes…His mercy and grace!

Who you are, where you have been, and what you've done can all be covered by the grace of God which enables you to make it.

By the grace of God you are what you are. However, grace does not stop there. Although grace is freely given, it confronts its recipients with an obligation—the obligation to allow God's grace to be manifested through them.

Grace provides us with everything that is Christ's. It makes us heirs of God and joint-heirs with our Lord Jesus Christ. Consequently, grace does not leave us inert or impotent. Grace is not inactive. This is why Paul says, "But by the grace of God I am what I am, and His grace toward me did not prove vain; but I labored even more than all of them, yet not I, but the grace of God with me" (1 Corinthians 15:10).

In Philippians 2:13 we saw that it is God who is at work in us both to will and to do His good pleasure. Ours is to say, "Jesus, be Jesus in me," as the song puts it, and to let His grace reveal itself as we reach out to others. Jesus is able to be "Jesus in you" because of the indwelling presence of the Holy Spirit.

Acts is an account of what happened when the Holy Spirit came to indwell believers. The grace and truth realized in Christ Jesus have continued down through the centuries as God's children have carried out to completion that which God was working in them by allowing the grace of God to labor through their lives.

When the apostles wanted to know when Jesus would restore the kingdom to Israel—i.e., when God's kingdom would be set up on earth as had been promised in Daniel 7 and in other Old Testament passages—Jesus replied, "It is not for you to know times or epochs which the Father has fixed by His own authority; but you shall receive power when the Holy Spirit has come upon you; and you shall be My witnesses both in Jerusalem, and in all Judea and Samaria, and even to the remotest part of the earth" (Acts 1:7-8).

They were looking for the kingdom; Jesus was telling them to occupy until He comes! One of the problems in Christendom today is that we have become occupied with trying to discern when He is coming instead of focusing on our responsibility to be about our Father's business, laboring in His grace.

Failure to allow His grace to labor through us in all of its power—this will be our greatest regret. Think on it.

− D A Y   T W O −

This week I want to look at several principles which will help you to say someday that God's grace was not poured out on you in vain.

First, Paul knew that we have access to the grace of God through faith in Jesus Christ. This is clearly stated in Romans 5:2.

1. Write out Romans 5:1-2.

The verb *stand* in the statement "in which we stand" is in the perfect tense. In Greek the perfect tense indicates that it is an action which took place in the past but which continues to be true. Thus, at salvation you and I were not only given access to the grace of God for that particular moment, but we stand there *right now*. Having access to the grace of God means that everything Jesus Christ is and everything He has is made available to you. The power of grace rests upon you.

This is why Peter exhorts the recipients of his first epistle the way he does.

2. Write out 1 Peter 5:12.

3. What is Peter exhorting his readers to do with respect to grace?

In the opening of his epistle, he wrote, "May grace and peace be yours in fullest measure" (1 Peter 1:2). It is one thing to have access to God's grace; it is another thing to appropriate it. Peter wrote his epistle to people who needed to understand suffering and, in the midst of their suffering, to remember how to relate to others—to those outside the faith, to those in positions of political power, to the elders of the church. He dealt with them on the relationship of slaves and masters, husbands and wives, the young and the old. Appropriating the grace of God in its fullest measure would enable them to serve God in an acceptable way.

To have God's grace and not appropriate it is to have it poured out on you in vain.

Think about it. Are you in a difficult relationship? God's grace is there. You have access to it. Allow Him to control you rather than being controlled by the circumstances of that relationship. Are you frustrated with governmental powers? Do you want to rebel? There is grace to enable you to "submit yourselves for the Lord's sake to every human institution" (1 Peter 2:13).

Are you living with an unsaved and difficult husband? There is grace. God says in 1 Peter 3:1 that if your husband won't obey the Word of God, you are to shut your mouth and win him by your behavior. That's hard…almost too much to bear. Yet, it's not impossible because you stand in the grace of God. Appropriate it. Do what 1 Peter 2:21–3:6 says, and leave your husband to God. Only God can change him.

I often tell a wife that it is not her responsibility to make her husband holy. Her responsibility is to try to make him happy. Only God can make him holy, and a wife should realize that she may not be able to make her husband happy. He might be as mean as a snake. At least she can rest in the fact that she tried and that she didn't compromise her relationship with God.

As a husband, are you frustrated with your wife, unable to understand her? There is grace to enable you to live with her in an understanding way and to honor her as you should (1 Peter 3:7).

Are you being mistreated by others because of your Christianity? There is grace to enable you to endure without returning insult for insult, evil for evil (1 Peter 3:8–4:19).

Is spiritual warfare wearing you down? Are you weary? There is grace to enable you to resist. "And after you have suffered for a little while, the God of all grace, who called you to His eternal glory in Christ, will Himself perfect, confirm, strengthen and establish you" (1 Peter 5:10).

When you stand firm in the grace of God, you serve God rather than self. Acceptable service unto God is manifesting His grace by the way in which you live. Therefore, keep in mind this first principle that will enable you to say that God's grace was not poured out on you in vain: *The child of God always has access to the grace of God; therefore, stand firm in it.*

— DAY THREE —

The second principle you need to embrace is this: *The grace of God provides you with spiritual gifts by which you are to serve the body of Jesus Christ.* As a steward of these gifts, you will be held accountable for using them.

Let's take a brief look at what the New Testament teaches on the subject of spiritual gifts. Look up the following verses and write out what you learn from each. Each time you see the word *grace* in any of these verses, you may want to mark it in a distinctive way in your Bible.

1. Ephesians 4:7-8

2. 1 Corinthians 12:4-7

3. 1 Corinthians 12:11 (Considering what you saw in verses 4-7, record what is distributed.)

4. 1 Peter 4:10-11

5. Romans 12:6

Now write out a summary statement of what you have learned about spiritual gifts.

How does what you have learned fit with the second principle I gave you at the beginning of today's devotional study? Write down your answer.

− D A Y   F O U R −

The grace of God puts us into God's "forever family." Within the family, each member is to serve God according to the grace God gives him. In the study you did yesterday, you saw that every believer has been given one or more spiritual gifts. These gifts are not given according to merit or desire. Rather, "God has placed the members, each one of them, in the body, just as He desired" (1 Corinthians 12:18).

When we received the Lord Jesus Christ, "by one Spirit we were all baptized into one body,...and we were all made to drink of one Spirit" (1 Corinthians 12:13). When this happens, God determines *where* we are placed in the body.

Every time God deals with the subject of spiritual gifts, He uses the analogy of the body. Why? Because the body is one entity. Yet, its members are diverse and function in unique ways for the proper working of the whole. Its various members illustrate what the Church of Jesus Christ is all about—unity in the midst of diversity—all under the headship of Jesus Christ.

As you saw in 1 Corinthians 12:4-7, the gifts, the ministries, and even the effects are all from the Godhead. God supplies us with everything we need in order to do what He has called us to do. This, my friend, is grace. Our gifts "differ according to the grace given to us" (Romans 12:6). And we are given grace "according to the measure of Christ's gift" (Ephesians 4:7).

And how does all of this fit into our study of grace—grace that is active and that labors? It is concisely stated in 1 Peter 4:10: "As each one has received a special gift, employ it in serving one another, as good stewards of the manifold grace of God."

Do you realize God has gifted you in a unique way so that you might serve Him? The first time I learned this truth I was writing a course on Romans. When I came to Romans 12:7—"Or ministry, let us wait on our ministering" (KJV)—I saw that we were to stay within the sphere of our gift.

My mouth dropped open. I couldn't stay within the realm of my gift if I did not know what my gift was! I began a study of the spiritual gifts by searching out everything the Bible had to say about the subject. What I learned became our Precept Upon Precept course on spiritual gifts.

May I urge you to think about these things. Remember, Beloved, God not only calls you to serve Him, but He gifts you so that you can.

— D A Y   F I V E —

Paul knew exactly what God had gifted him to do. He knew it, and he served God and the body of Jesus Christ within the framework of his gifts. Thus, the grace of God labored through him.

When Paul was imprisoned in Rome, he wrote the following words to the church at Ephesus. Read them carefully. Watch for the words *grace*, *minister*, and *power*, and underline them.

❱ EPHESIANS 3:7-8

7 of which I was made a minister, according to the gift of God's grace which was given to me according to the working of His power.

8 To me, the very least of all saints, this grace was given, to preach to the Gentiles the unfathomable riches of Christ.

Now take these two short verses and examine them asking the "5 Ws and an H." Write out all you learn by asking these questions, but don't add anything to the text.

Grace for service. It was uppermost in Paul's mind. Read what he wrote to the church at Rome: "Jesus Christ our Lord, through whom we have received grace and apostleship to bring about the obedience of faith among all the Gentiles, for His name's sake" (Romans 1:4-5).

Paul realized that in the grace of God he had been called to be an apostle. It didn't matter to him that he was "the least of the apostles." He would not refuse to serve God if he could not be foremost. Instead, he would appropriate God's grace to the fullest. There would not be one measure of grace that Paul would not use up.

This brings us to the third principle: *With the grace of God comes a specific purpose for your life.* Ephesians 2:8-10 says, "For by grace you have been saved through faith; and that not of yourselves, it is the gift of God; not as a result of works, that no one should boast. For we are His workmanship, created in Christ Jesus for good works, which God prepared beforehand, that we should walk in them."

1. In the light of these verses, what do you learn about the purpose for your life?

2. How would you tie these verses in with what you learned about spiritual gifts?

When Paul knew his ministry on earth was coming to a close, he wrote one last letter to Timothy, his son in the gospel. In that letter Paul exhorted Timothy to kindle afresh the gift of God which was in him, reminding him that God has not given us a spirit of timidity, but of power and love and discipline.

Listen to his word of exhortation. As you read, watch for the words *purpose* and *grace.*

Therefore do not be ashamed of the testimony of our Lord, or of me His prisoner; but join with me in suffering for the gospel according to the power of God, who has saved us, and called us with a holy calling, not according to our works, but according to His own purpose and grace which was granted us in Christ Jesus from all eternity. (2 Timothy 1:8-9)

3. What do you learn about the calling of God in a Christian's life?

   In 2 Timothy 1:11-12, Paul writes:

   …for which I was appointed a preacher and an apostle and a teacher. For this reason I also suffer these things, but I am not ashamed; for I know whom I have believed and I am convinced that He is able to guard what I have entrusted to Him until that day.

4. What had God, in grace, appointed Paul to do?

5. According to these verses, why was Paul able to serve God even though he suffered?

6. Are you able to do the same, even though you suffer? Why?

7. If Paul hadn't served God even though he suffered, what would that tell you about Paul's attitude or response to the grace of God?

8. Beloved, what has been your response to the grace of God?

Aren't you as responsible as Paul?

— D A Y   S I X —

This is the fourth and final principle of grace: *Grace is activated by faith.*

It is one thing to stand in the grace of God and to be gifted by God for the work of ministry. It is another thing to live in the light of these facts. This is where faith comes in. Faith activates or releases the grace of God.

Grace strips all people of their need for anything but humility. Then it gives to the humble a vault of all the treasures and resources of God. However, that vault is only unlocked with the key of faith. That's why so many of God's children are powerless.

First, they have not humbled themselves under the mighty hand of God. Instead, they have listened to messages and books which exalt man. They have been seduced into a "pseudo" faith which centers on what we believe about ourselves and our own human potential and capability.

Second, they do not understand biblical faith. Their faith is placed on what they believe about God rather than on the whole counsel of the Word of God. However, the certainty of faith is found not in the believer but in who and what is believed. If we believe in what we say, our faith rests in ourselves. If we believe what God says—*in the context of the whole Bible*—our faith rests in the infallible Word of God and in the character of God. "For Thou hast magnified Thy word according to all Thy name" (Psalm 138:2). "According to" can be translated "together with." God is saying that if the Word fails, His name fails. Therefore, the Word of God stands because God stands by His Word.

O Beloved, on what are you basing your faith? Your words, your desires, your beliefs? Are you part of so many who are saying, "I claim that by faith"? If so, on what basis are you claiming it?

I become so distressed when I receive letters from people who think God has forsaken them because they have not received what they claimed by faith. And how I grieve over those who write me and request a book, tape, or even a personal letter giving them counsel from God's Word and then say that they can't send me any "seed faith money" because they're broke. But they assure me that they will when they can, if I'll only help them. I just want to cup their faces in my hands and say, "Read my lips carefully. God is not like that. You don't have to give to God's servants in order to get from God."

He's a God of grace. Remember that, my friend, and trust in His Word, not in your faith. When you trust in His Word, He will honor your faith.

— D A Y   S E V E N —

Let me say it again so that you don't miss it: Grace strips all men of their need of anything but humility, and grace opens to the humble a vault of all the treasures and resources of God which we unlock with the key of faith. Grace and faith cannot be separated. We cannot lay hold of grace apart from faith.

By faith we totally rely on God, rejecting confidence in ourselves and placing our confidence in who God is and in what He says. This is how we are to live in every situation of life. Think with me for a moment, and you will see what I mean.

When we sin as children of God, what makes us right with God? Must we do penance? Sacrifice something? Promise that we will never do it again? You know the verse already. God says, "If we confess our sins, He is faithful and righteous to forgive us our sins and to cleanse us from all unrighteousness" (1 John 1:9). How can God do this? Grace. Yet, what releases this grace? Faith that acts on what God says in 1 John 1:9. If we don't handle our sin God's way, it will affect our service for God.

When you encounter trials that you feel will overwhelm or destroy you, how can you survive without losing your faith or your mind? You must believe that His grace is sufficient for any and every circumstance of life. The minute you believe, the power of grace is released. All of this is taught in 2 Corinthians 12, and we will look at it in depth in our final week of study. Just remember that if you do not appropriate in faith God's all-sufficient grace in the trials of life, it will affect your service for God. Without appropriating His grace, your trials can overwhelm you or consume your thoughts, thereby distracting you from God's calling upon your life.

When you encounter failure and you feel there is no way to recover from your mistakes, what will keep you from drowning in the quicksand of despair? What will keep you from bitterness, anger, or lashing out? God's grace which promises that all things will work together for good. Appropriate it.

O Beloved, do you see that it's one thing to have access to the grace of God but another to appropriate it? Notice that I said "appropriate." Grace can never be earned or merited. It can only be believed, appropriated by faith. "*The* righteousness of God is revealed from faith to faith; as it is written, 'BUT THE RIGHTEOUS man SHALL LIVE BY FAITH'" (Romans 1:17). The Christian life begins with faith, is lived by faith, and is maintained by faith. It is all of faith.

"Therefore, since we receive a kingdom which cannot be shaken, let us show gratitude, by which we may offer to God an acceptable service with reverence and awe" (Hebrews 12:28).

MEMORY VERSE

For in it the righteousness of God is revealed from faith to faith; as it is written, "BUT THE RIGHTEOUS man SHALL LIVE BY FAITH."

ROMANS 1:17

SMALL-GROUP DISCUSSION QUESTIONS

In week seven we discussed the apparent contradiction that the grace of God is available for every situation and yet we can look at some Christians who do not seem to be as effective as other Christians. When we reflect on the state of Christendom, we may wonder why the kingdom of God does not progress more expediently. We looked at scriptures that helped us to understand that we are the bottleneck, that we need to work out our salvation.

We looked at the way Paul responded to the grace of God in his life, and we realized that he could have let his past overcome him had he not understood and appropriated the grace of God.

Then finally we looked at Psalm 139 to get a perspective on our God and His understanding of us, and we came to an even better understanding of His graciousness toward us through this study.

1. What obligation does grace carry with it?
2. How are we able to fulfill this obligation?
3. What gives us access to the grace of God?
4. What does it mean to have access to the grace of God? How will this understanding affect you moment by moment?
5. When would God's grace be poured out on you in vain?
6. In His grace, what has God provided you so that you can serve the body of Jesus Christ?
7. What purpose do the gifts serve?
8. Are all of these gifts alike? Do they all have the same result?
9. How is it determined which gift(s) you will receive? When do you receive the gift(s)?
10. In your study this week, what did you learn about the purpose of your life?
11. Will you be able to serve God no matter what He brings into your life? Why? Share the example of this from Paul's life.

12. We all have access to the grace of God, but what activates the grace of God?
13. By what are we able to unlock all the resources of God which He has made available to us?
14. Grace strips us of everything except what?
15. What gives faith its strength?
16. What is necessary in order to lay hold of grace?
17. If you do not appropriate the grace of God, how can this affect your service for Him?
18. What did you learn this week about grace and faith that will change your perspective forever?
19. What spiritual gift have you been given to serve the body of Christ? In which ministry do you use your gift? (Don't feel bad if you don't know; just determine before God to find out by studying His Word and by waiting on Him to show you.)

MY TRIALS SEEM OVERWHELMING

— *D A Y   O N E* —

Grace does not exempt us from trials; it takes us through them. No matter what you are suffering, dear child of God, God's grace is sufficient. This is the message of 2 Corinthians 12:9.

Through the centuries it's a promise that has buoyed up Christian after Christian in trial after trial. Right after I became a believer, I was introduced to many of these saints of old. When I use the term *saint*, I'm not talking about someone who has been canonized by a church. I am using the biblical synonym for a child of God. Because every child of God has been sanctified by our Lord Jesus Christ, all Christians are saints.

Let's go to the Word so you don't just take my word for it. Look up the following verses and watch for the words *saint* and *sanctified*. Both words come from the same Greek root *hagios*, which means "set apart." As you read, record what you learn about Christians.

a. Hebrews 10:10

b. Romans 1:6-7

One saint who weathered the storm, proving the sufficiency of His grace, was Jeanne Marie Bouvier de la Motte. She lived during the long and extravagant reign of Louis XIV. Madame Guyon, as she was later called, was born on April 18, 1648.

Madame Guyon was to become a thorn in the flesh of her king, who lived in debauchery. Born into nobility, this tall, exquisite beauty caught the attention of the courts of France at a very early age. Her presence was demanded at every party and social event...and it was her pleasure to be the center of attention. She knew what went on in those inner circles because for a while she was part of them. Everything in Paris catered to her pride. And yet Jeanne Marie's soul had been awakened to the things of God. Because her mother was more concerned with social affairs and caring for her favorite charities than with raising her daughters, Jeanne Marie had been sent off to a convent when she was only two and a half years old.

The dichotomy of lifestyles pulled at her conscience. Finally the Lord won, and Madame Jeanne Guyon fell in love with the One who died for her. That love would be tested repeatedly in fires of suffering which would be kindled time and time again for the rest of her life. Yet, each fire only consumed more dross. Her flesh was left in the ashes, and the gold of her relationship with her Savior gleamed in an ever-greater purity.

Her pen became a sword, slashing through the sin of the times, revealing many of the heretical teachings of the church. Her fame spread throughout Europe. But not everyone was happy with her writings. Many of the church prelates were infuriated. Louis XIV winced, writhed, and then came to the end of his endurance.

Madame Guyon was imprisoned far below the surface of the earth. Her cell was lit only by a candle, but she still had pen and paper. After ten years in her dungeon, bent low over the linen parchment on the table, squinting as the candle flickered in the draft, she moved her quill across the paper to write this poem. It has survived the centuries not only as a testimony to the sufficiency of God's grace, but also as a monument to the certainty of His promise that He will not give us anything we cannot bear.[1]

A little bird I am shut from the fields of air
Yet in my cage I sit and sing to Him who placed me there;
Well pleased a prisoner to be,
Because my Lord, it pleases Thee.

Nought else have I to do, I sing the whole day long.
And He whom most I love to please
Doth listen to my song.
He caught and bound my wandering wing, but still He bends to hear
     me sing.

My cage confines me round, abroad, I cannot fly
But though my wing is closely bound, my heart's at liberty.
My prison walls cannot control the flight, the freedom of the soul.

Ah, it's good to soar these bolts and bars above,
To Him whose purpose I adore, whose providence I love
And in Thy mighty will to find the joy, the freedom of the mind.[2]

O Beloved, are you convinced that if God's grace were not sufficient, the trial could not come? God has given us a wonderful promise which we need to keep ever before us in times of difficulty. Interestingly enough, He also gave it to the Corinthians through Paul:

No temptation has overtaken you but such as is common to man; and God is faithful, who will not allow you to be tempted beyond what you are able, but with the temptation will provide the way of escape also, that you may be able to endure it. (1 Corinthians 10:13)

Therefore, Beloved, when you suffer, you must remember the following: First, *it is not more than you can bear.*

Second, *God has a way of escape.* The way of escape is not to run from the trial or circumstance. You must take God's way of escape, not yours. Today so many people have an unbiblical concept of trials, suffering, and God. They cannot imagine a God of love allowing one of His children to suffer. This thinking shows ignorance of the whole counsel of God.

We are not only to believe on Jesus Christ, but also to suffer for His name's sake (Philippians 1:29-30). God uses trials to bring us to Christlike maturity. Everywhere trials are discussed—from Romans to James to 1 Peter—you see this message. Look up the following verses and note what they have in common. You might want to write out the verses and underline the parallel words or phrases, or you may want simply to record the commonalities.

1. Romans 5:3-5

2. James 1:2-4

3. 1 Peter 1:6-7

In each of these incidents, we are told to endure, to abide under—to *hupomenø,* as the Greek puts it.

So when you look to God for "the way of escape," make sure that it is *His* way of escape, not your way or your rationalization of His way. He will hold you accountable.

And remember, it is one thing to grit your teeth, to bear your trials and say, "Well, I guess His grace'll be sufficient." It is another thing to rejoice as each of these passages says we are to do. We need to say with Paul, "I am well content with weaknesses, insults, distresses, persecutions, and difficulties." When you say the latter, you prove that you know that His grace is sufficient.

My friend, where do you stand? Where do you want to stand? Can you? Why? How? Write it out.

− D A Y   T W O −

How we would love to soar above our problems and distresses! And yet, grace lets us plod rather than soar blissfully above it all. Such was the life of William Carey, a cobbler turned missionary.

After a long life of enduring great and plentiful hardships, he wrote: "If anyone should think it worth his while to write my life, if he give me credit for being a plodder he will describe me justly. I can plod. I can persevere in any definite pursuit. To this I owe everything."[3]

Grace enabled Carey to plod. It was William Carey who coined the phrase that has endured since the late 1700s, echoing over and over again the sufficiency and power of God's grace: "Expect great things from God. Attempt great things for God."

These words were preached to lethargic Christian leaders who had ignored and then forgotten Christ's commission to go into all the world and preach the gospel to every creature. Into his sermon Carey "poured all the longings of his heart for over eight years. Over and over he repeated the phrase—"Expect great things from God. Attempt great things for God"— until it sank into the hearts of those who heard. The words came from the soul of the preacher and spread across his listeners with the impact of an explosion. They were jolted out of their lethargy as the Holy Spirit moved among them. It was the era of long and ponderous sermons, but this time the address was short and simple. This was a burning bush of missionary enterprise, calling to the listless churches of the day to enlarge their tents, to lengthen their self-centered cords, to widen their vision.

"Carey told them: 'God is calling you to a brilliant future, to preach the gospel throughout the world. My friends, you need this wider vision.'"4 They needed it. But for years, only he would heed it. They looked at the task and were overwhelmed. "What can a mere handful of preachers accomplish?" They had failed to consider the grace of God which takes a mere man and accomplishes the work of God through him!

Do you wonder the same thing? Put it away. File your doubts under the grace of God. If you cannot soar with eagle's wings, plod on in faith.

Although Carey's message stirred men's hearts, it did not move them to action. Carey walked away. The church leaders resolved to send missionaries to foreign shores but nothing more. They listened but didn't act.

Carey plodded on in the grace of God, formulating the plan himself. A year later at their annual October gathering, the Missionary Society finally agreed to send Carey to India. Little was known about this country fifteen thousand danger-ridden miles away.

Carey's dilemma now was his wife, Dorothy. Dare he ask this simple and unlearned woman to take their children and go with him? Was it right to ask her to make such a sacrifice? If he had to go without them, it would mean death to his happiness. But if that was his only alternative, then he determined that was the way it would have to be. He had to be willing to forsake all, even his wife's desires, if he had to make a choice between obedience to his Lord and his own happiness.

When Carey reached home and told Dorothy of his plans, she refused to uproot her family. No one could persuade her to do otherwise. The torment of soul was almost overwhelming. Carey's faith hung by a thread, but it held, and he determined to go to India without his wife.

Even Carey's father thought him mad when he received his son's letter: "I hope, dear father, you may be enabled to surrender me up to the Lord for the most arduous, honourable, and important work that ever any of the sons of men were called to engage in. I have many sacrifices to make. I must part with a beloved family and a number of most affectionate friends…. But I have set my hand to the plough."5

Nothing but the Word of God could call him to this sacrifice. Grace would have to sustain him as he plodded on in faith. Only if God Himself provided a "ram in the thicket," as He did for Abraham, could there be any deviation in the sacrifice.

When God calls us to a task, He never deprives us of the grace we need!

Look up, write out, and memorize Mark 10:29-30 (also read verse 28).

— D A Y   T H R E E —

God's grace held Carey when it seemed impossible to raise the money for his trip, when the pain of the impending separation from his wife and children pierced his heart, when it became difficult to find a captain of a ship who would take him as a passenger.

The East India Company did not want missionaries spoiling their business by proclaiming the gospel to the heathen. There was delay after delay as promises were broken and captains were intimidated. Thomas, a man who had lived in India and wanted to return as a missionary under their Society, was to travel with Carey.

As they prepared to sail, another crushing blow came down on Carey's faith. The captain of the ship suddenly got cold feet. Fearing the East India Company's reprisals, he told Thomas and Carey that he would only take Thomas's wife and daughter to India.

Their plans had fallen through again. As Carey watched the ship sail without him, he could not help but cry out, asking God what on earth He was doing. Would he never reach India?

Then the tide began to turn. Word came to Carey and Thomas of passage that could be booked at a greatly reduced price. Excited, they set off together to see Carey's family:

> Carey…returned to Portsmouth and took the coach to London. There was news from home that the expected baby had arrived and he now had another son. He had written to his wife: "If I had all the world I would freely give it all to have you and the children with me." With this unexpected change of plan there might be an opportunity to see them all once more.
>
> William lifted the latch of the cottage door and walked in; it was no wonder Dorothy looked, gasped, and burst into tears. She was dreaming. She must be. A dream that was too good to be true! Then surprise gave place to delight, and eagerly she fetched the new baby to meet his father.
>
> As Dorothy's sister Katherine prepared a hurried breakfast for them all, Carey took the opportunity to appeal to his wife once more. They prayed together but Dorothy was still too afraid to take what seemed to be such a dangerous step into the dark.
>
> When the time came to say good-bye, the two men…set out…. Carey was so overcome with grief at the parting that after a few miles

Thomas, whose sympathetic nature could not bear to see it, decided they must return and make one more effort.

Dorothy's loving heart could stand no more, and in tears she said she would go if her sister would go too. Taken aback by this sudden turn of events, Katherine had only a few minutes to make up her mind. She sent up a quick prayer for guidance.

Early in the morning of June 13th, 1793, the whole family went aboard the sailing ship *Kron Princessa Maria* and all hundred and thirty feet of her length seemed to Carey as pure gold. This was the ship that was to take not only himself, but his wife and children, across the vast ocean to an unknown land. He was at last on his way to a people he already loved because of their need, and to a work that was dearer to him than life itself.[6]

Upon arriving in India, Carey encountered one trial after another. His money dwindled because Thomas spent their whole year's allowance in their first ten weeks in India. His missionary efforts were violently opposed and threatened by the government. He sought employment and housing for his homeless family who were already plagued with dysentery and homesickness.

Little did this missionary realize that it would be seven years before he would see his first Indian convert. On that day Dorothy did not stand at his side. She was confined to her room, mentally ill. Carey did not realize her condition either. All he knew was that God's grace is sufficient and that His power is perfected in our weakness.

He would need to know this truth, to remember it always, because eleven years of mission work would take the lives of seven of his colaborers who followed him to India, including Thomas. For the next twenty-three years, only three of them would be left to carry on the work "as a three-fold cord, each depending on the others and drawing strength from that fellowship. They became known as the 'Serampore Triad.'"[7]

Carey again found God's grace sufficient and his trials not more than he could bear. Then in 1812 tragedy struck and fire destroyed the Serampore Press and much of Carey's translation work. He wrote: "The loss is heavy, but as traveling the road a second time, however painful it may be, is usually done with greater ease and certainty, so I trust the work will lose nothing in real value.... The work is already begun again in every language."8

In 1833 fever and weakness caused him to be confined to a chair placed on two boards and rolled around on four wheels. Then the day came when he was confined to his home. Still, this harvester of grace plodded on, going over the final proofs of his Bengali New Testament. Then,

> as the sun rose into a cloudless sky on the morning of June 9th, 1834, the pioneer reached the last rung of the ladder. As he entered into the eternal presence of the Author, in his hand was the new edition of the Bengali New Testament.
>
> India had said good-bye to one of her greatest benefactors, and on the Danish Government House at Serampore the flag was seen to be flying at half-mast.9

When Carey was confined to his room, a man among a group of visitors spoke glowingly of Carey's accomplishments. When the time came for the man to leave, Carey said softly, "Mr. Duff, you have been talking much of Dr. Carey. When I am gone, say nothing about Carey. Speak instead of Carey's Saviour."10

It's all of grace—grace sufficient, grace that will not give you more than you can bear.

Don't you love stories like that? There's so much we can learn from them. These were people who understood and lived in the grace of God. Review what you have seen in Carey's life. What have you learned that you can apply to your life? Write out the principle.

Can you say with Paul and with Carey, "By the grace of God I am what I am, and His grace toward me did not prove vain…" (1 Corinthians 15:10)?

O Father, may Your grace in my life not be in vain. May I ever draw from its sufficiency, and may I ever serve You in its power. I pray this for myself and for those for whom I labor in writing this study. I ask it all through the grace given to me in Your Son, my Lord and Savior Jesus Christ.

— D A Y F O U R —

When things don't go our way, when our happiness is threatened, when God isn't giving us what we want, when we don't think our needs are being met, there is a great temptation to take the easy way out, to turn back to our old ways, to yield to our flesh, or to give up in discouragement.

This is the feeling the recipients of the letter to the Hebrews were experiencing. They didn't understand that the trials they were enduring were part of God's discipline. And so in the eleventh chapter of his word of exhortation, the author of Hebrews reminded them of their need of faith. He spoke to the fact that things are not over, that the drama of redemption has not yet come to an end. He encouraged them to remember that if they wanted God's approval, they must continue in faith.

"Now faith is the assurance of things hoped for, the conviction of things not seen. For by it the men of old gained approval." And with that introduction, the author reminded them of the men of old and their walk of faith—faith that endured although they "did not receive what was promised" (Hebrews 11:1-2,39).

Then, pointing back to the "so great a cloud of witnesses," the writer exhorted them to "lay aside every encumbrance, and the sin which so easily entangles us, and…run with endurance the race that is set before us, fixing our eyes on Jesus, the author and perfecter of faith, who for the joy set before Him endured the cross, despising the shame, and has sat down at the right hand of the throne of God" (Hebrews 12:1-2). What they were encountering was known by God. It was His discipline to refine them further, to free them from encumbrances and sins which were keeping them from His likeness. Once again the readers were directed to look to the throne.

Throughout the pages of this exquisite letter to the Hebrews, we are constantly reminded that we have access to God's throne of grace. Jesus, our Great High Priest, has passed through the heavens. Therefore, we must hold fast our confession and "draw near with confidence to the throne of grace, that we may receive mercy and may find grace to help in time of need" (Hebrews 4:16).

Like you and me, they needed to remember that grace does not exempt us from suffering and trials, it sees us through them. Our responsibility is to avail ourselves of the grace which flows from His throne.

In their suffering and trials, the writer gives them the following reminder:

❶ HEBREWS 12:5-17

⁵ and you have forgotten the exhortation which is addressed to you as sons,

"MY SON, DO NOT REGARD LIGHTLY THE DISCIPLINE OF THE

LORD,

NOR FAINT WHEN YOU ARE REPROVED BY HIM;

⁶ FOR THOSE WHOM THE LORD LOVES HE DISCIPLINES,

AND HE SCOURGES EVERY SON WHOM HE RECEIVES."

⁷ It is for discipline that you endure; God deals with you as with sons; for what son is there whom his father does not discipline?

⁸ But if you are without discipline, of which all have become partakers, then you are illegitimate children and not sons.

9 Furthermore, we had earthly fathers to discipline us, and we respected them; shall we not much rather be subject to the Father of spirits, and live?

10 For they disciplined us for a short time as seemed best to them, but He disciplines us for our good, that we may share His holiness.

11 All discipline for the moment seems not to be joyful, but sorrowful; yet to those who have been trained by it, afterwards it yields the peaceful fruit of righteousness.

12 Therefore, strengthen the hands that are weak and the knees that are feeble,

13 and make straight paths for your feet, so that the limb which is lame may not be put out of joint, but rather be healed.

14 Pursue peace with all men, and the sanctification without which no one will see the Lord.

15 See to it that no one comes short of the grace of God; that no root of bitterness springing up causes trouble, and by it many be defiled;

16 that there be no immoral or godless person like Esau, who sold his own birthright for a single meal.

17 For you know that even afterwards, when he desired to inherit the blessing, he was rejected, for he found no place for repentance, though he sought for it with tears.

1. Read through this passage from Hebrews 12 again and mark the following words in a distinctive way.

a. holiness, righteousness (Mark these in the same way.)
b. discipline
c. grace

2. List everything you have learned about the discipline of the Lord from this passage. Put your information under the appropriate heading.

WHO IS DISCIPLINED?

WHY ARE THEY DISCIPLINED?

WHAT IS TO BE THE RESULT OF DISCIPLINE?

HOW ARE THEY TO RESPOND?

WHAT CAN HAPPEN IF THEY DO NOT RESPOND
PROPERLY?

Think on these things, and we will discuss them more tomorrow.

— *D A Y   F I V E* —

The birthright of every child of God is grace—grace that saves and sustains, grace that will keep us and bring us to glory.

Yet, with our birthright comes responsibility. We are responsible to have faith. We must believe that God means what He says and stands by His Word. The grace that has saved us to salvation is sufficient to take care of us. We cannot say that we accept that grace, cast it away in unbelief, and return to life apart from it when the going gets rough. If this scenario is played out, we despise our birthright. Apart from grace there is no hope.

The author of Hebrews illustrates this mind-set in the account of Esau in Genesis 25 and 27. When Esau came in from the fields, he was famished. "And Esau said to Jacob, 'Please let me have a swallow of that red stuff there, for I am famished.' Therefore his name was called Edom. But Jacob said, 'First sell me your birthright.' And Esau said, 'Behold, I am about to die; so of what use then is the birthright to me?' And Jacob said, 'First swear to me'; so he swore to him, and sold his birthright to Jacob. Then Jacob gave Esau bread and lentil stew; and he ate and drank, and rose and went on his way. Thus Esau despised his birthright" (Genesis 25:30-34).

Esau looked at the temporal, his fleshly needs, rather than at the eternal, his birthright. In the midst of a trial, he yielded to the flesh and sold his birthright for a bowl of stew! Esau reverted to the flesh. He looked at today instead of tomorrow, and he lived for today. He despised his birthright.

When we fall back on the flesh during times of trouble or trials, we come short of the grace of God. And as Hebrews says, a "root of bitterness" can spring up in us and defile others. Or we can become immoral or godless like Esau, who sold his birthright for a single meal (Hebrews 12:15-16).

O Beloved, you profess to know the Lord. You say that you have been saved by His grace. Beware of despising the birthright which belongs to every child of God. Realize that suffering is part of God's fatherly discipline which belongs to every child of God. He disciplines us for our good. His goal is that we become holy, or as He puts it in Hebrews, that we might share in His holiness.

– D A Y   S I X –

When you suffer, remember that you have a place to run—the throne of grace.

> For you have not come to a mountain that may be touched and to a blazing fire, and to darkness and gloom and whirlwind, and to the blast of a trumpet and the sound of words which sound was such that those who heard begged that no further word should be spoken to them.... But you have come to Mount Zion and to the city of the living God, the heavenly Jerusalem, and to myriads of angels, to the general assembly and church of the first-born who are enrolled in heaven, and to God, the Judge of all, and to the spirits of righteous men made perfect, and to Jesus, the mediator of a new covenant, and to the sprinkled blood, which speaks better than the blood of Abel.... Therefore, since we receive a kingdom which cannot be shaken, let us show gratitude, by which we may offer to God an acceptable service with reverence and awe; for our God is a consuming fire. (Hebrews 12:18-19,22-24,28-29)

When you act on God's grace, when you trust God's purposes during trials, the reality of the grace of God spreads because others see the reality of Christ and His sufficiency in us. Therefore, "we have this treasure in earthen vessels, that the surpassing greatness of the power may be of God and not from ourselves; we are afflicted in every way, but not crushed; perplexed, but not despairing; persecuted, but not forsaken; struck down, but not destroyed; always carrying about in the body the dying of Jesus, that the life of Jesus also may be manifested in our body" (2 Corinthians 4:7-10).

Have you ever seen your trials and suffering from this perspective? They are not without purpose. Nor will they destroy you. As you appropriate His all-sufficient grace, suffering and affliction become your platform for the reality of Christ. Thus, Paul goes on to say, "For we who live are constantly [Did you note "constantly"?] being delivered over to death for Jesus' sake, that the life of Jesus also may be manifested in our mortal flesh. So death works in us, but life in you.… For all things are for your sakes, that the grace which is spreading to more and more people may cause the giving of thanks to abound to the glory of God" (2 Corinthians 4:11-12,15).

Paul's sufferings were God's means of spreading His grace to others. Your suffering will do the same thing if you stand firm in His grace. You may not see it now, but when you stand before His throne, you will. This truth has been confirmed from one generation to another. It is recorded in the annals of church history. *When the saints suffer, it is never in vain.*

The blood of the martyrs is the seedbed of the gospel. Why? Because those without Christ realize that if they were in the Christian's shoes, they would probably behave differently. As we appropriate God's grace, they see us "in no way alarmed by [our] opponents—which is a sign of destruction for them, but of salvation for [us], and that too, from God" (Philippians 1:28).

Grace takes us *through* suffering. Remember, we are afflicted, *but not crushed;* perplexed, *but not despairing;* persecuted, *but not forsaken;* struck down, *but not destroyed.* The way we suffer shows the difference between us and the lost. The difference is the grace of God—grace that not only saves us but sustains us, sufficient for every need, every trial.

– D A Y   S E V E N –

So often we quote Romans 8:28, but we don't take time to look at it in its context. If you want to see how and why God's grace is sufficient in all your trials, then it would be good for us to look at Romans 8:28-39. Read it through carefully, and then I'll ask you some questions which will help you better understand the text.

And we know that God causes all things to work together for good to those who love God, to those who are called according to His purpose.

For whom He foreknew, He also predestined to become conformed to the image of His Son, that He might be the first-born among many brethren; and whom He predestined, these He also called; and whom He called, these He also justified; and whom He justified, these He also glorified. What then shall we say to these things? If God is for us, who is against us? He who did not spare His own Son, but delivered Him up for us all, how will He not also with Him freely give us all things? Who will bring a charge against God's elect? God is the one who justifies; who is the one who condemns? Christ Jesus is He who died, yes, rather who was raised, who is at the right hand of God, who also intercedes for us. Who shall separate us from the love of Christ? Shall tribulation, or distress, or persecution, or famine, or nakedness, or peril, or sword? Just as it is written,

"FOR THY SAKE WE ARE BEING PUT TO DEATH ALL DAY LONG; WE WERE CONSIDERED AS SHEEP TO BE SLAUGHTERED."

But in all these things we overwhelmingly conquer through Him who loved us. For I am convinced that neither death, nor life, nor angels, nor principalities, nor things present, nor things to come, nor powers, nor height, nor depth, nor any other created thing, shall be able to separate us from the love of God, which is in Christ Jesus our Lord.

1. According to this passage what is God's goal for you as His child?

2. Does God say that all things are good? Explain.

3. How does someone really know that God is for him?

4. According to this passage, what do the Father and Son do for the believer?

5. Why suffering?

6. How can a child of God handle suffering?

7. Is suffering a sign that God doesn't love us? Explain your answer.

8. What did you learn from this passage that you can personally apply to your life?

Suffering is never wasted—it is used to make us more like Christ and, as a result, causes the grace of God to spread, and God is glorified. Thus, Paul explains our suffering: "FOR THY SAKE WE ARE BEING PUT TO DEATH ALL DAY LONG; WE WERE CONSIDERED AS SHEEP TO BE SLAUGHTERED" (Romans 8:36). It will help to remember, my friend, that your sufferings are for His sake, endured by His grace!

I believe it will also help you to look at the Author and Finisher of your faith and remember "the grace of our Lord Jesus Christ, that though He was rich, yet for your sake He became poor, that you through His poverty might become rich" (2 Corinthians 8:9). No matter what your sin, your weaknesses or inadequacies, your sufferings or the cost of Christ-likeness, the grace of God has made you rich in Jesus.

Now, Beloved, as we bring this study to a close, my prayer is that "grace and peace be multiplied to you in the knowledge of God and of Jesus our Lord; seeing that His divine power has granted to us everything pertaining to life and godliness, through the true knowledge of Him who called us by His own glory and excellence" and that you "grow in the grace and knowledge of our Lord and Savior Jesus Christ" (2 Peter 1:2-3; 3:18).

"And now I commend you to God and to the word of His grace, which is able to build you up and to give you the inheritance among all those who are sanctified…. To this end also [I] pray for you always that our God may count you worthy of your calling, and fulfill every desire for goodness and the work of faith with power; in order that the name of our Lord Jesus may be glorified in you, and you in Him, according to the grace of our God and the Lord Jesus Christ" (Acts 20:32; 2 Thessalonians 1:11-12).

MEMORY VERSE

Let us therefore draw near with confidence to the throne of grace, that we may receive mercy and may find grace to help in time of need.

HEBREWS 4:16

SMALL-GROUP DISCUSSION QUESTIONS

In week eight our study centered on the grace of God poured out in our lives.

We looked again at the fact that the grace of God is activated and appropriated by faith. We saw, too, that our faith is only as strong as the object in which we have placed it.

A new insight that we gained last week was that we have each been given a spiritual gift(s) by which to serve the body of Christ. We saw that by using this gift we were appropriating the grace of God through faith in service to our brothers and sisters.

We also understood that grace could be poured out on us in vain, and we talked about how to be certain that this would not be the case in our lives.

1. What did you learn about grace from the passage in 2 Corinthians 12 that you studied this week?
2. Are we never to suffer trials, sufferings, heartaches because we belong to the Lord?
3. If trials do come, what assurance do we have in the midst of them?
4. Does God ever place us in a trial or in a time of suffering that we are not able to handle? How do you know?
5. What does the scripture mean when it says that God will provide the way of escape in any temptation?
6. Can you explain the sufficiency of His grace for every trial of life? How is His grace sufficient?
7. What purpose do trials serve in our lives?
8. Again, you saw the relationship between power and grace. Can you explain it? What does that mean for you?
9. From what you saw this week in Hebrews, why are we disciplined?
10. What is the result of the discipline of the Lord?
11. In the discipline process, what is our responsibility?

12. What can happen in the midst of a trial if we do not respond properly?

13. Grace is a free gift of God to His children. But what is our responsibility regarding grace?

14. What was Esau's mistake in his trial? What lesson can we learn from the way he responded?

15. Where are we to run when we find ourselves in the midst of a trial?

16. When we respond properly in a trial, what effect does it have on others?

17. What will carry us through the trial, the suffering?

18. How will you respond the next time you find yourself in the midst of a trial, in suffering?

19. As you enter into a trial, what verse do you need to remember and keep ever before you?

20. What have you learned this week about the discipline of the Lord?

STUDY

RESOURCES

HOW TO MARK YOUR BIBLE

O ne of the things we at Precept Ministries International teach you to do in inductive Bible study is to find the key words in the passage you're studying and to mark them in a distinctive way. This is a very helpful and important element of the essential Bible study step known as observation—discovering exactly what the text says. So many times a Scripture passage is misinterpreted simply because the initial work of accurate observation has not been done. Remembering to mark key words will help you not to overlook this critical step.

WHAT ARE KEY WORDS?

Key words or phrases are those that are essential to the text. If they were to be removed, you would find it difficult or impossible to grasp the essence of what the passage is about. Like keys, these words "unlock" the meaning of the text. Recognizing them will help you uncover the author's intended purpose and emphasis in his message.

Key words can be nouns, descriptive words, or action words. Very often an author will repeat these words or phrases in order to emphasize his message. They may be repeated throughout an entire book—like the key words *love* and *abide,* which we see throughout the book of 1 John. Or they may be repeated throughout a shorter section of text, as with the key word *fellowship,* which is used four times in the first chapter of 1 John but not elsewhere in the book.

In the "Lord" series of Bible studies, you will often be asked to find and mark certain key words or phrases in the passage you're studying. This is a method that you will want to make a lifelong habit in your personal Bible study.

HOW TO MARK KEY WORDS

Marking key words can be done in several ways.

1. You can use different colors or a combination of colors to highlight

different words. When I mark a passage, I like to choose a color that to me best reflects the word I'm marking. I color references to God in yellow because God is light and in Him there is no darkness. I color sin brown. Any Old Testament reference to the temple is colored blue.

2. You can use a variety of symbols—simply drawing a circle around a word, underlining it, or marking it with a symbol of your own creation, such as these:

When I use symbols, I try to devise one that best pictures the word. For example, the key words *repent* and *repentance* in Matthew 3 might be marked with the symbol since in Scripture this word's root meaning represents a change of mind, which often leads to a change in direction.

3. You can combine colors with symbols. For example:

- In 1 John 3, the key word *love* could be marked with a red heart like this: If you want to distinguish God's love from man's, you could color God's heart yellow and man's red.
- Every reference to the devil or evil spirits could be marked with a red pitchfork.
- Every occurrence of covenant could be colored red and boxed in with yellow.

The *New Inductive Study Bible* (NISB) has a whole page of suggested markings for key words used throughout the Bible.

A WORD OF CAUTION

When looking for key words, sometimes the tendency is to mark too many words. For example, I rarely mark references to God and to Jesus Christ unless it is significant to understanding the message. For instance, the phrases "in Christ" and "in Him" are significant to understanding the message of Ephesians 1–3. If you marked every reference to Jesus in some of the gospel accounts, your Bible would be too marked up. So you need to use discretion. (I always mark every reference to the Holy Spirit because He is not referred to often, and there is much confusion about the person and ministry of the Holy Spirit.)

Remember to look for those words that relate to the foundational theme of the text. Sometimes a key word may not be repeated frequently, but you know it is key because without it you would not know the essence of what the author is talking about in that passage.

BE SURE TO MARK KEY-WORD SYNONYMS AND PRONOUNS

Synonyms for a key word would be marked the same way you mark the key word. For example, you would mark identically the word *devil* and the phrase "evil one" in Ephesians 6:10-18.

And be sure to mark pronouns (I, you, he, she, it, we, our, and so on) the same way you would mark the words to which they refer. In 1 Timothy 3:1-7, for example, you would mark the pronouns *he* and *his* in the same way you did the key word *overseer* in that passage.

For consistency, you may want to list on an index card the key symbols and colors you like using for certain words and keep that card in your Bible.

IMMEDIATE IDENTIFICATION

With a passage's key words marked in this way, you can look at the text and immediately spot the word's usage and importance. In the future you'll quickly be able to track key subjects and identify significant truths in any passage you've studied and marked.

CREATE LISTS FROM KEY WORDS

After you mark key words, you will find it helpful to list what you learn from the text by the use of the key word. For instance, once you mark the word *sin* in 1 John 3, you would make a list of what the text tells you about sin. As you look at each marked key word, list anything that would answer the questions *who, what, when, where, why,* or *how* about sin. You will be not only surprised but also delighted at the truths you can learn from this simple process of observation.

For more on how to mark your Bible and on the inductive Bible study approach, you may want to use the *New Inductive Study Bible* (from Harvest House Publishers), or you can reach us at Precept Ministries International by referring to the contact information in the back of this book.

GUIDELINES FOR GROUP USE

This study book, as well as all those in the "Lord" series, can be used for home Bible-study groups, Sunday-school classes, family devotions, and a great variety of other group situations. Here are some things to keep in mind as you use this study in a group setting to minister to others.

- Prayerfully commit the entire study to the Lord, seeking His direction for every step.

- As your group forms, encourage each member to purchase an individual copy of this book.

- If you have the companion audio or videotapes for this course, begin your first class by listening to or viewing the introductory lesson on the study. Each student should then do the study preparation for chapter 1 before the next class. (Encourage each student to faithfully do this week by week.)

- Beginning with your next meeting, your weekly pattern as you meet should be to first discuss what you have all studied and learned on your own during the preceding week. Then, if you so desire, you could have a teacher present an in-depth message on the material you just studied. Or you could listen to or watch on video the teaching tapes available on this series. Just make sure that the teaching tape follows the class discussion rather than precedes it. You want your group to have the joy of discovery and discussion.

- The group discussion questions following each chapter in this book are to aid you in leading a discussion of that week's material. However, merely having these questions will not be enough for a really lively and successful discussion. The better you know your material, the greater freedom you will have in leading. Therefore, Beloved, be faithful in your own study and remain dependent upon the ministry of the Holy Spirit, who is there to lead you and guide you into all truth and who will enable you to fulfill the good work God has fore-ordained for you. (As the group's leader, it would be ideal if you could either read the entire book first or do several weeks' study in advance, so you know where you're going and can grasp the scope of the material covered in this study.)

• Each week as you prepare to lead the group's discussion, pray and ask the Father what your particular group needs to learn and how you can best cover the material. Pray with pen in hand. Make a list of what the Lord shows you. Then create your own questions or select from the questions at the end of each chapter, which will help stimulate and guide the group members in the Lord's direction within the time you have.

• Remember that your group members will find the greatest sense of accomplishment in discussing what they've learned in their own study, so try to stick to the subject at hand in your discussion. This will keep the class from becoming frustrated. Make sure the answers and insights come from the Word of God and are always in accordance with the whole counsel of God.

• Strive in your group to create an atmosphere of love, safety, and caring. Be concerned about one another. Bear one another's burdens and so fulfill the law of Christ—the law of love (Galatians 6:2). We desperately need one another.

Please know that I thank our Father for you and your willingness to assume this critical role of establishing God's people in God's Word. I know that this process produces glory and reverence for Him. So press on, valiant one. He is coming, bringing in the kingdom in all its glory, and His reward is with Him to give to each one of us according to our deeds.

THE "LORD" SERIES: AN OVERVIEW

My burden—and calling—is to help Christians (or interested or desperate inquirers) see for themselves what the Word of God has to teach on significant and relevant life-related subjects. So many people are weak and unstable in their Christianity because they don't know truth for themselves; they only know what others have taught them. These books, therefore, are designed to involve you in the incomparably enriching experience of daily study in God's Word.

Each book has been thoroughly tested and has already had an impact on a multitude of lives. Let me introduce the full series to you.

Lord, I Want to Know You is a foundational study for the "Lord" books. In this seventeen-week study you'll discover how God's character is revealed through His names, such as Creator, Healer, Protector, Provider, and many more. Within the names of God you'll encounter strength for your worst trials, comfort for your heart's deepest pain, and provision for your soul's greatest need. As you come to know Him more fully—the power of His glorious name and the depth of His infinite love—your walk with God will be transformed and your faith will be increased.

Lord, Heal My Hurts is, understandably, one of the most popular studies in this series. If you're in touch with the world, you know that people around you are in great pain. We run to many sources for relief when we are in pain. Some of us turn to other people; many escape into drugs, work, further education, and even hobbies. But in God you can find salvation from any situation, from any hurt. In this thirteen-week study you'll see that, no matter what you've done or what's been done to you, God wants to become your refuge…He loves you and desires your wholeness…and He offers healing for your deepest wounds.

Lord, I Need Grace to Make It Today will reveal to you in fresh power the amazing truth that God's grace is available for *every* situation, no matter how difficult, no matter how terrible. You'll gain the confidence that God will use you for His glory, as His grace enables you to persevere regardless of your need, regardless of your circumstances, and despite the backward pull of your flesh. You will see and know that the Lord and His all-sufficient grace will always be with you. A highlight of this nine-week course is your study of the book of Galatians and its liberating message about our freedom in Christ.

Lord, I'm Torn Between Two Masters opens your understanding to the kind of life that is truly pleasing to God. If you've known discouragement because you felt you could never measure up to God's standards or if you've ever felt unbearably stretched by the clash of life's priorities, this nine-week study of the Sermon on the Mount will lead you into a new freedom that will truly clear your vision and fortify your heart. You'll be encouraged to entwine your thoughts, hopes, dreams, and desires around heavenly things, and you'll find your life transformed by choosing to seek first God's kingdom and His righteousness.

Lord, Only You Can Change Me is an eight-week devotional study on character that draws especially on the so-called Beatitudes of Matthew 5. If you've ever been frustrated at not being all you wanted to be for the Lord or at not being able to change, you'll find in this study of Christ's teaching the path to true inner transformation that is accomplished only through the work of the indwelling Holy Spirit. You will learn the achievable reality of a godly life and the fulfillment it can bring.

Lord, Where Are You When Bad Things Happen is a critically important study in preparing you for times of trial. In this ten-week course you'll be grounded in the knowledge and confidence of God's sovereignty as you study especially the book of Habakkuk and see how God works in and through difficult and demanding situations. More than that, you'll learn what it means to live by faith…and to rest the details of your life in His hands.

Lord, Is It Warfare? Teach Me to Stand is a study that trains you for spiritual battle. God's Word tells us that our adversary, the devil, goes about like a roaring lion seeking whom he may devour (1 Peter 5:8). Many times we either don't recognize this enemy, or we're scared by his roar. We would like him to go away, but it's not that simple. In this eleven-week study you'll learn how to recognize Satan's tactics and how to be set free from bondage. As you focus your study especially on the book of Ephesians, you'll discover how to build an unshakable faith that makes victory yours for the taking. (This is the most challenging of the "Lord" books and requires an average of two to two and a half hours of weekly preparation to complete the assignments.)

Beloved, I have written these books so that you can have insight from God's Word on the pertinent issues of life—not only for yourself, but also for your ministry to others.

Know that you are on my heart because you are precious to God and I long to see you live as more than a conqueror, fulfilling God's purpose for your life.

ON-LINE RESOURCES

A s you plant the seeds of God's Word in your heart in this study, I want you to know that you can now find immediate encouragement and help in a variety of ways just by connecting to our special "Lord" studies Web site at the address listed below.

Here's a sample listing of what you'll find at this site:

- Helpful information for guiding your individual study in this and other "Lord" books
- More detailed information on the exact study focus in all the "Lord" books
- Guidelines for group leaders and facilitators, both to get your group started and to keep it functioning in the best way
- Group study questions for you to download and reformat in a way that is most helpful for you and your group
- Additional insights on the topics in the "Lord" studies from the Precept Ministries International team
- Opportunities for you to join others in sharing your discoveries from God's Word

This information is continually updated to ensure that we're offering you the best support possible. Please e-mail and let us know what you find most helpful from this "Lord" studies Web site!

For more information on this and other "Lord" studies:
www.lordstudies.com
For other resources and information from Precept Ministries International:
www.precept.org

NOTES

CHAPTER ONE

1. From time to time we will look at the definition of a word in the Greek or Hebrew. Since the Old Testament was originally written in Hebrew, and the New Testament was originally written in Koine Greek, sometimes it is helpful to go back to the original language to see the meaning of a word. There are many study tools to help you if you would like to do this type of digging. One excellent book to help you understand how to do more in-depth study is *How to Study Your Bible* (Harvest House Publishers, 1994).
2. James Orr, ed., *The International Standard Bible Encyclopedia,* vol. 2 (1939; reprint, Grand Rapids, Mich.: Eerdmans, 1976), 1292.
3. Lawrence O. Richards, *Expository Dictionary of Bible Words* (Grand Rapids, Mich.: Zondervan, 1985), 317.

CHAPTER THREE

1. William J. Petersen, *Johann Sebastian Bach Had a Wife* (Wheaton, Ill.: Tyndale House, 1987), 25.
2. Petersen, *Bach Had a Wife,* 29-30.
3. Petersen, *Bach Had a Wife,* 30, 33.

CHAPTER FOUR

1. John Pollock, *A Fistful of Heroes: Great Reformers and Evangelists* (London: Marshall Pickering, 1988), 87-88. Used by permission.
2. Pollock, *A Fistful of Heroes,* 90-91.

CHAPTER FIVE

1. Petersen, *Bach Had a Wife,* 35-36.
2. Orr, *The International Standard Bible Encyclopedia,* 1292.
3. Orr, *The International Standard Bible Encyclopedia,* 1291.
4. Kenneth Wuest, "Treasures from the Greek New Testament," *Word Studies in the Greek New Testament,* vol. 3 (Grand Rapids, Mich.: Eerdmans, 1973), 16, citing Trench, *Synonyms of the New Testament.*

CHAPTER NINE

1. Paraphrased from Dorothy Gawne Coslet, *Madame Jeanne Guyon: Child of Another World* (Fort Washington, Penn.: Christian Literature Crusade, 1984). Used by permission.
2. Poem by Madame Guyon. Printed source unknown.
3. Kellsye M. Finnie, *William Carey: By Trade a Cobbler* (Kent, England: Send the Light, 1986), 25. Used by permission.

4. Finnie, *William Carey,* 48.
5. Finnie, *William Carey,* 56.
6. Finnie, *William Carey,* 62-65.
7. Finnie, *William Carey,* 110.
8. Finnie, *William Carey,* 125-130.
9. Finnie, *William Carey,* 152.
10. Finnie, *William Carey,* 151.

About Kay Arthur and Precept Ministries International

Kay Arthur, executive vice president and cofounder of Precept Ministries International, is known around the world as a Bible teacher, author, conference speaker, and host of national radio and television programs.

Kay and her husband, Jack, founded Precept Ministries in 1970 in Chattanooga, Tennessee. Started as a fledgling ministry for teens, Precept today is a worldwide outreach that establishes children, teens, and adults in God's Word, so that they can discover the Bible's truths for themselves. Precept inductive Bible studies are taught in all 50 states. The studies have been translated into 65 languages, reaching 118 countries.

Kay is the author of more than 120 books and inductive Bible study courses, with a total of over 5 million books in print. She is sought after by groups throughout the world as an inspiring Bible teacher and conference speaker. Kay is also well known globally through her daily and weekly television and radio programs.

Contact Precept Ministries for more information about inductive Bible studies in your area.

Precept Ministries International
P.O. Box 182218
Chattanooga, TN 37422-7218
800-763-8280
www.precept.org